ENJOY YOUR GOLF

THE SECRET OF GOOD GOLF

by MEL FLANAGAN

i

Dedicated to my wife Imelda.

Rozanna, Robbie, Elizabeth,
Melvyn, Lisa, Lucy & Rosie.

ACT AS IF YOU ALREADY ARE A GOOD GOLFER!

To really enjoy golf, you must have inner confidence. Quietly remind yourself that you are a good player, that you enjoy the game, that you like practising, that you have a great short game. Always wish the very best to your opponents. Be big. Play the course rather than your opponent. Encourage your playing partner and wish him/her well. Compliment them on a good shot. If you are a beginner you should study etiquette. A lot of it is common sense - respect for your golfing friends and for the golf course. Become a brisk player. Don't be too hard on yourself! - as a beginner, when you are not playing in competitions, tee the ball up if you are out on the fairway.

Acknowledgement

I would like to thank Derick Turner, Gillian O'Neill and
Lorna McGoey of Turners Print, Longford.

My wife and family. Also Gerry Gregg and all who helped.

INTRODUCTION

I was once asked by a researcher for the late late what is the secret to the game. I was stunned into complete silence by the simplicity of the question. For many years I pondered the subject . I have watched thousands of golfers travel towards the first tee with fear in their eyes. This fear of "failure and hope for success" was always going to work against them.

Now and again golfers would ARRIVE on a different planet always dressed to kill with beautiful equipment. They laughed even at the poorest of jokes. They seemed to ceremoniously "levitate" towards the first tee. One of them remarked to me "you know I have a special routine. I always use a very long white wooden tee (no plastic for him), I reverse the number on the ball (always a pro v) so I can chicken eye it" and he continued "you would not believe this. I HUMM to myself on my back swing, IT'S IMPORTANT TO REALISE and at the top of my back swing I pause for a split second and say "THAT' On my down and through swing "NOTHING IS REALLY IMPORTANT " I said I do not believe you he replied "watch" and so demonstrated out loud this time. I eliminate the "fear of failure or the pressure of success" as neither is important to me at this time.

These special golfers are always great company. They radiate relaxation .... And Success. Members often commented 'I always play better with him' These golfers in fact discovered the secret OF the game TO ENJOY IT.-. To totally participate from the inside out. To explore this further it is interesting to note that as the PHYSICALITY of the game decreases up and around the green the mental stress increases.

A Brother of mine an excellent golfer at the Rossespoint club was asked by the barman "why the two glasses of beer" when he was sitting alone in an empty clubhouse he replied "I always buy a drink for my good friend MY PUTTER. It holed so many putts for me today". Yet so many of us hate our putters and criminalize our clubs. We often comment, "I must get rid of that club and buy one that works. Think of the golfer whose only fear is that his favourite club might be stolen. My brother often comments "the ball operates almost as if it had a jockey on it directing it down the golden line (note the happy golfer always bestows success on to the putter and away from himself).

Finally I cannot leave you without sharing with you an EXPERIENCE I had. I was watching a Hitchcock film - I have often wondered why you will always hole a putt on the second attempt. In the film a young man arrived into the foyer of the hotel. He was full of life. It was in the smoking "era". He flicked his cigarette lighter. An older man approached (JOHN HOUSTEN) he challenged him with "I bet you cannot do it nine times in a row" the young man said no problem "watch" - Houston interrupted "no I mean a real bet. Come upstairs to my apartment". The next scene- Houston says, "look out the window and you will see that beautiful red Ferrari parked on the street down below. If you are successful I will give it to you - His girlfriend urged caution saying, "There must be a catch"... Houston interrupted saying "there is, if the lighter fails to light on any of your nine attempts I can chop off one of your fingers!. The final scene - a weird looking female accomplice of Houston holding a very large menacing knife over the young mans hand as it was tied to the table with Houston looking on. The young man was torn between the fear of the knife and the hope of winning the Ferrari. This purely mental conflict inside his head prevented him from doing anything. Success and failure were now totally dominant, the second chance putt is of no consequence (similar to the young man on the ground floor without any knife or Ferrari fear), and that's why you always hole it. The fear you encounter on the first tee and green is totally self-inflicted. You are operating outside the PRESENT. Golf is hounding you. Your new resolution must be and make it right now. I AM GOING TO ENJOY MY GOLF FROM THE FIRST TEE TO THE FINAL PUTT. As Kipling once said of success and failure 'TREAT THOSE TWO IMPOSTORS MUCH THE SAME"

CONTENTS

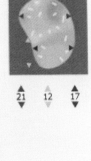

18 31 21

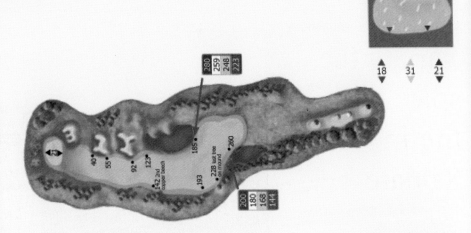

280 259 248 223

185 260

40 55 92 123

142 2nd copper beech

228 last tree on mound

193

200 180 168 144

RATH HILL

Par 5
502 481 469 444 **13**

21 12 17

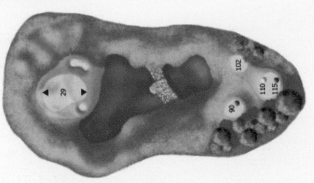

102

110 115

29

90

SPRING

Par 3
130 125 116 105 **15**

X

THE IRISH TIMES

Course Development Dunmurry Springs

Variety the spice of life in rural Kildare

Philip Reid pays a visit to Dunmurry Springs, another fascinating new golf club in a county which is rapidly becoming a Mecca for the game.

The concept is not a new one, transforming agricultural pastures into a golf course. As a foreign friend enquired recently, "is there no part of Ireland that won't eventually be a golf course?" And, certainly, the growth over the past decade or so has been remarkable.

What is different about Dunmurry Springs is the terrain has guaranteed a different kind of examination and course designer Mel Flanagan, while keeping to traditional values, has ensured that variety is the spice of life.

Built on hills just off the winding road that links Kildare town with Rathangan, Dunmurry Springs - so called because the limestone-based terrain is blessed with natural springs, which have been utilised to create a number of impressive and aesthetic water hazards - is an 18-hole course in the final stages of readiness.

The plan is to allow restricted play to members from October, but the full opening won't take place until the spring. By then, the clubhouse, due to start construction shortly, will have been completed.

Sensibly, though, the onus has been on developing the course first before the bricks and mortar element of the development. What has materialised in the fields once farmed by the Holohan family is a course that, thankfully, is not a beast in terms of length - it will play to under 7,000 yards - and yet asks enough questions of a player to be a tough examination.

Flanagan, who has established a nice portfolio of courses as a course architect, is particularly pleased with what has unfolded at Dunmurry Springs on land he described as "like an awkward child in a classroom," adding: "It was an awkward site to work with, but the result is a course where every hole gives the golfer a sporting chance."

The idea for the golf course evolved over a number of years and came from the golf playing father and son partnership of Seán and Simon Holohan.

"Our objective was to create a golf course of outstanding quality on what is a very special site," explained Seán.

Indeed, for the first-time visitor, the real surprise is that such a hilly site should be found in the plains of Co Kildare. From the highest point, by the fifth green, the vista is a breathtaking one that offers a view of no fewer than eight counties.

With an investment in excess of €7 million, it was a project that wasn't entered into lightly but the Holohans, having researched its viability, have left no stone unturned in their efforts to establish a niche in the market.

The intention, when the course opens in the springtime, is for visitors to be offered a genuinely warm welcome.

"We want to take away any stuffiness or aloofness that is sometimes associated with golf," said Una Holohan, the sales and marketing manager.

As evidence that there has been no short-cutting, some 2,000 semi-mature trees of between 20 and 25-years-of-age have been transplanted onto the course.

They include indigenous Irish trees of beech, ash and oak and complement the mature trees and hedgerows.

What has materialised is a course - share memberships are currently on offer at €12,500 in this latest tranche - that will appeal to many in Kildare, a county that is increasingly becoming a Mecca for the game.

The first hole is a par four that rises gently uphill and, indeed, Flanagan has succeeded admirably in using the terrain. Although hilly, the layout - which has two loops of nine - is such that there is no undue physical exertion and the first hole is a gentle introduction that certainly whets the appetite.

The front nine comprises of seven par fours, one par five - the sixth - and one par three, the seventh. There is tremendous variety on this stretch, with the second a dogleg that requires accuracy off the tee and the third a beautiful downhill hole to a green that is protected by a pond and which has an old tradesman's cottage as a backdrop.

"My idea was to give people a chance to get into the game, by offering some gentle opening holes, before asking the really tough questions," said Flanagan.

It is a concept that works well. And the stretch of holes from the sixth to the eighth is particularly impressive.

These were the first holes to be sown, back in May/June, and the advances in agronomy are such that you'd swear the fairways and greens have been here for many years.

The conditioning is a tribute to course superintendent Gerard McEvoy, who previously worked at the Heritage and assisted with the grow-in of the West Course at Powerscourt, and his assistant Ciarán Blackburne, who returned from the Hills Golf Club in Sweden to take up the position at Dunmurry Springs.

The sixth is a par five that doglegs to the right. It is a fine test, requiring a long and accurate drive with out-of-bounds down the right and mounding that blends in with the surrounding countryside down the left. The approach is uphill to a green that is the highest point on the course and is followed by the only par three on the outward run.

The hole is played from an elevated tee to a green that is guarded by bunkers which the designer has built to penalise.

"The bunkers are real bunkers," said Flanagan, with no apology. "I've gone back to the old style bunker where you won't get out unless you play a golf shot."

The eighth hole is a wonderful test, with the fairways framed by impressive mounding on either side. It is a hole reminiscent of the heath land courses at Gleneagles, with ample gorse and lovely, undulating fairways that could leave a player with an uphill or a downhill lie for the approach to a green surrounded by bunkers.

Flanagan has also provided a number of holes where he challenges the player to open his shoulders off the tee, and the ninth is one of them. From an elevated tee, the tree-lined fairway is sufficiently wide to tempt the big-hitters to unwind and the approach is then played to a green that is fronted by an impressive lake. Indeed, all of the lakeside greens have fabulous stonework built into them, which certainly add to the aesthetics of the course.

The last three holes to be grown in are the 10th, 11th and 12th - which comprise a mini-loop around a couple of lakes that take you back towards where the clubhouse area will be situated.

The par three 11th has the potential to be one of the trickiest holes on the course.

In fact, each of the par threes (there are three of them on the back nine) is particularly nice and the 15th, which is played almost entirely over a lake, is sure to break many a heart.

"This is not a big slog of a course, a player will always have a chance - but he has to play the shots, otherwise the course will punish," said Flanagan.

"It's challenging, but it is fair . . . it's a real golfer's course."

> '**MY** idea was to give people a chance to get into the game, by offering some gentle opening holes, before asking the really tough question'
>
> **-Mel Flanagan**

Clockwise: *Melvyn Flanagan,*
John Daly & Mel Flanagan

Mel Flanagan outside
'Hotel The Flanagan'

Blarney Golf Course

Pat Flanagan, Mel Flanagan,
Mick Faldo & Melvyn Flanagan

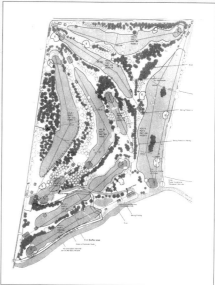

Clockwise: *Mel Flanagan at 'St. Oswalds Golf Course, Austria'*

Thurles Golf Club, Conceptual Layout 'Hole 1 to 9'

An aerial view of what could be one of the greatest golf courses in the world - Bartra Island

Frank McCarthy, John Daly, Mel Flanagan & John Kelly Proprietor of Blarney Golf Course

GETTING STARTED

THE RIGHT APPROACH

Improving your golf takes time, patience and effort. The fact is, you may initially play a lot worse before you improve! You must be prepared for this.

It is worth remembering the following points:

Adopt a positive attitude

Decide that you are going to become a great player. Act as if you already are a great player. Adopt an 'improving' mentality. Continually imagine yourself striking the ball well. Repeat these words to yourself many times: 'I am a good player', 'I love the game', 'I enjoy practising'.

It is very important that you associate with positive-minded golfers who think like yourself. Avoid negative thinkers. They are everywhere. Do not let the negative attitudes of others destroy your plans for success. Even the way you dress is important. Make no mistake about it, how you look on the outside affects how you feel. If you dress well, you will automatically feel well and play better. Great players all have economy of movement in their swings — they dress neatly, tidily and are very organised. You are what you think you are. Use clothing as a tool to lift your spirits, to build confidence.

Practise to play, don't play to practise

New techniques must be practised. You should not try to digest large amounts of information and then head out onto the golf course with the intention of putting it to the test in your game. This will be disastrous, as on the course you will have only *one* shot with a whole lot depending on it, and probably three impatient golfers waiting for you. So forget it — practise first!

Beat time!

One of the greatest problems in teaching golf is the fact that players never seem to have time to practise between lessons. They are always too busy. You must never allow this to happen to you. Use time in every conceivable way. A simple point — you do not have to be on a practice ground in order to practise. You can practise as you are reading this book! Have a club beside you (preferably an 8 Iron) and work on it as you see the concept that appeals to you. In this way you are schooling yourself to do the basic movement correctly. Your muscles and

Fig 1.1 Practise your swing at home in front of a mirror.

brain will learn together, until the movement becomes 'muscle memory' and your swing instinctive.

Be prepared for setbacks, but wait for the 'magic moments'

A curious fact about the way we progress — when we start to learn anything, especially golf, we never advance steadily. We do not improve gradually. We do it by sudden jerks, by abrupt starts. Then we remain stationary for a time, or we may even slip back and lose some of the ground we had previously gained. These periods of stagnation or retrogression are normal and have been named 'plateaux in the course of learning'. Potentially good golfers will sometimes be stalled for weeks on one of these plateaux. They may be practising hard but cannot get past this brick wall. The weak ones give up in despair. Those with true grit persist, and they find that suddenly, overnight, without their knowing how or why, it has happened, they have made great progress. They have lifted from the plateau like an aeroplane. Abruptly they have found the knack. Have the patience to wait for these magic moments!

Good things do not happen by accident! I have for many years observed golfers practising — those who have succeeded are not as a general rule players of extraordinary ability. Rather, they have been endowed with persistence and dogged determination. They kept on. They arrived.

Go 'first class' on your equipment
Pay twice as much — buy half as many. Buy clubs that complement your game.
Remember, the Driver is a very important club. I see so many people with totally unsuitable Drivers, so rigid, heavy and straight-faced that even tournament players would have trouble breaking 80 with them.

Fig 1.2 When buying your Driver, bear in mind that you can gain extra distance if the shaft is flexible.

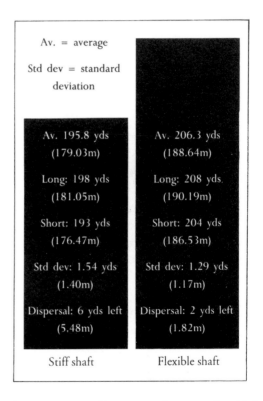

Av. = average	
Std dev = standard deviation	
Av. 195.8 yds (179.03m)	Av. 206.3 yds (188.64m)
Long: 198 yds (181.05m)	Long: 208 yds (190.19m)
Short: 193 yds (176.47m)	Short: 204 yds (186.53m)
Std dev: 1.54 yds (1.40m)	Std dev: 1.29 yds (1.17m)
Dispersal: 6 yds left (5.48m)	Dispersal: 2 yds left (1.82m)
Stiff shaft	Flexible shaft

An easy-to-use Driver is what you should be looking for — one that is lofted, light, and not too stiff in the shaft. The lightness will make it easy to swing, the whippier shaft will add extra distance, and the loft will keep the ball on line by creating back-spin rather than side-spin.

Do not fall into the trap of doing your final exam first

I always remember a player who came to me in the driving range and said: 'I want to learn the game of golf.' I noticed he had only one club with him — a Driver. I enquired if he had any other clubs. He said no. His theory was simply this: the Driver is the most difficult club, so if he mastered that one, the rest would come easy. I explained to him the perils of 'trying to do the final exam first', that he wasn't in the range for exercise, rather to learn a basic technique.

Forget about results (for a while), and other peoples expectations.

Do not let people intimdate you!

EQUIPMENT

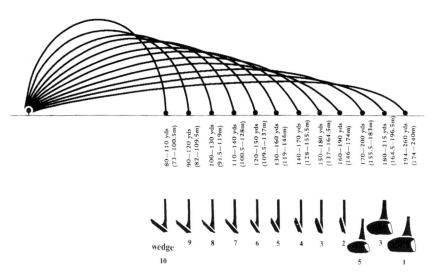

80–110 yds (73–100.5m)	90–120 yds (82–109.5m)	100–130 yds (91.5–119m)	110–140 yds (100.5–128m)	120–150 yds (109.5–137m)	130–160 yds (119–146m)	140–170 yds (128–155.5m)	150–180 yds (137–164.5m)	160–190 yds (146–174m)	170–200 yds (155.5–183m)	180–215 yds (164.5–196.5m)	194–260 yds (174–240m)	

wedge   9   8   7   6   5   4   3   2   3

10   5   1

Fig 1.3 This diagram shows the distances that both professional and handicap golfers can expect to achieve with individual clubs.

Clubs

You are allowed only fourteen clubs. The choice of clubs is entirely up to yourself.

The Woods generally run from No. 1 to No. 5, the Irons from No. 2 to Sand-wedge (No. 11).

The Woods from No. 1 to 5, and the Irons from No. 2 to 6 are the really difficult clubs to use. A Driver or No. 1, unless made to order, has an 11 degree loft; the face is very flat.

You should look at the markings on the sole plate of the Woods and by the lines you will know if you are an 'out to in' or an 'in to out' swinger. You could double check this by looking at the Irons, and from the markings on the face you will see what part of the club 'meets' the ball. You should also look at the Woods and check the paint to see if you are using a steep swing and chipping the paint on the top of the head. Pupils never believe me when I tell them that they are hitting the ball near the shank of the Iron. I mark the back of the ball with chalk, and this chalk mark is transferred onto the clubface at impact. Immediately they can see if it's too near the shank of the clubhead. You should try this experiment for yourself.

The golf-ball

In my opinion, despite the advertising claims, there is not much difference in the distance you will get from balls of comparable quality. Tests conducted by the US Golf Association showed that no brand is appreciably superior to its several nearest competitors.

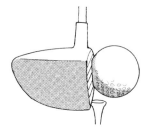

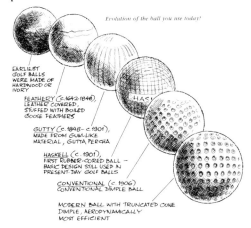

Evolution of the ball you use today!

EARLIEST GOLF BALLS WERE MADE OF HARDWOOD OR IVORY

FEATHERY (c.1642-1848), LEATHER COVERED, STUFFED WITH BOILED GOOSE FEATHERS

GUTTY (c.1848 - c.1901), MADE FROM GUM-LIKE MATERIAL, GUTTA PERCHA

HASKELL (c.1901), FIRST RUBBER-CORED BALL - BASIC DESIGN STILL USED IN PRESENT-DAY GOLF BALLS

CONVENTIONAL (c.1906) CONVENTIONAL DIMPLE BALL

MODERN BALL WITH TRUNCATED CONE DIMPLE, AERODYNAMICALLY MOST EFFICIENT

Fig 1.4 The distance a ball will travel is determined by the strength of impact between clubhead and ball.

The distance a ball will carry is governed by how much it is compressed and its ability to snap back when struck. This will depend on how hard the ball is and how hard it is struck. To increase your driving distance, think of compressing the ball a little bit more than you normally do at impact.

Modern balls range from 100 compression to 60. 100 is suitable for hard hitters, while average players should use 80 to 90. Compression increases in cold conditions and decreases in heat. This is why you should play with a softer ball in the winter.

A golf-ball may not weigh more than 1.62 ounces (45.92g) or be less than 1.68 inches (4.26cm) in diameter.

The earliest golf-balls were made of hardwood or ivory. These were followed by balls stuffed with feathers, and later by the gutta percha ball, filled with a rubber-like substance. Later balls had rubber liquid or steel centres wound up with stretched rubber bands and balata (a type of gum). Today golf-balls are solid and cut-proof. Aerodynamics of 336 dimples and back-spin of from 2000 to 8000 r.p.m. (revolutions per minute) keep the ball airborne for twice as long as a ball with a smooth surface.

The speed with which the ball leaves the face of the Driver when struck by a good golfer is about 170 m.p.h (273.5 km.p.h). The high-compression ball is in contact with the clubface for 4/10,000 of a second. The softer ball stays on the clubface longer and, therefore, it can be controlled better.

UNDERSTAND THE BASICS

Grip 'softly' and swing 'easy'

Look at the grip on the shaft of the clubs. The markings on the grip will reveal if the club is moving too much in your swing. If you are wearing your grips a lot, you are gripping the club too tightly, swinging too much with your hands and too fast. Your game will improve a lot if you respect your grips. It is important not to 'strangle' the club with your hands. No matter how lightly you hold the club it will always 'firm' up when the ball goes down and you make a swing at it. On the other hand, if you grip very tightly at address, it will ease on the take-away. It will always be a fast right side take-away which immediately loosens at the top, and you will lose control through the hitting area.

The cure is to grip very loosely as if the club was going to 'fly' out of your hands, and practise hitting half the distance with a full swing. Feel your arms are swinging, not just your hands and wrists. In other words, move your whole left side back while you keep your strong right side quiet on the backswing.

Fig 1.5 Tightening your grip will <u>not</u> result in greater distance.

Avoid the 'V' swing

To solve the mystery of golf, you must understand the geometry involved. What is the first aim of the swing? What are you trying to do? The first aim of your golf swing is to move the ball forwards — down the fairway.

The force or power of your swing with the club must be applied from 'behind', towards the back of the ball. This seems easy, but it is actually very difficult to do. Why?

1. We have to stand on one side of the ball (over it) as we prepare to move it forwards. We are in a very steep position over the ball at address. We would much prefer if we were allowed to stand behind it.

Fig 1.6 Avoid the 'V' swing. This illustration demonstrates the effect of the 'V' swing, and the more acceptable wide sweeping swing. The wide swing doubles your distance.

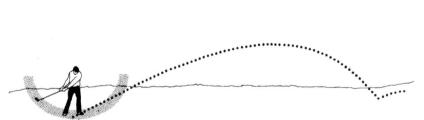

2. Unfortunately we make the ball the 'focal' point of the swing. As we swing the club farther back, we inevitably swing it higher and higher, so as we change direction and swing forwards, a major thought in our mind is to strike a good shot. What we are concentrating on is the ball on the

ground. The actual clubhead has reached a height of six feet (almost 2m) at the top of the backswing. Many golfers take the direct route down, straight down — the 'V' swing. This is much easier to do. What we *should* do is 'bottom' the clubhead first, then swing it forwards. Swing wide and easy into the back of the ball. Do not swing directly to the ball from the top. Do not swing 'at', swing 'through' the ball.

3. The right-hand side of your upper body is more developed, which lends itself to a stronger right-hand grip and a lifting action — steep backswing.

4. We associate a long drive with power. We grip tighter and snatch the club with hands and wrists only — a 'lottery' swipe at the ball.

In the driving range, many golfers practise mistakes — usually one or other variety of the 'V' swing.

THE 19th

The 'correct' golf swing

Let us look at what happens in other sports in a dead-ball situation, for example, converting a try in rugby or taking a corner kick in soccer. Let us study the action, the angles that are used.

The player, once he has placed the ball on the ground, goes back at an 'inside angle' and runs in from this 'inside angle'; he swings his foot from an inside-out angle as he strikes the ball. He does not run straight back and would never consider an outside run.

A good golf swing uses similar angles. I call it the 'L' turn. A backward and forward movement. A bald factual statement. At

John Daly

Staying behind yet
" releasing the clubhead"

address you stand ABOVE a golf-ball. You must school yourself to swing BEHIND the ball, at a slight angle — like the rugby or soccer player — and on swinging forwards, always swing the clubhead in shallow from behind and extend your arms on the follow-through. Wide, Wide, Wide!

The difference between the good and the bad swing is simply that in the bad swing the clubhead is descending sharply on the ball, while in the good swing the clubhead is sweeping in along to the ground.

Turn the 'L' and break out of the 'V' forever. Look after the 'middle' of your swing.

On the practice ground:
Have a short-range attainable goal, for example, a 100-yard (90m) accurate shot.

Use an 8 Iron, tee the ball up, use a very short swing. Above all, grip lightly and hit the ball softly. 'Caress' the little ball down the fairway.

▶ GOOD SWING THOUGHTS — repeat to yourself:

'No wrists. Dead hands.'

'I know I am standing *above* the ball.'

'I am going to turn *behind* the ball.'

'I am going to strike the *back* of the ball.'

'I am going to move *through* the impact area.'

'I am going to extend my arms out after impact, ensuring a *wide* follow-through.'

Reading ball flight

The height of your shots is dictated by your plane of swing.

If your shots are too high, your swing plane is steep. You are contacting the ball much too low, coming down on it. This steepness creates excess back-spin, causing the ball to rise up very high and drop down a short

Fig 1.8 A steep swing causes low contact, and this creates excessive back-spin and a high shot.

distance away. So the height is due to the angle of your attack or the actual part of the ball you strike — top, middle, bottom.

If your swing-plane is too flat (rounded), your shots will fly much too low, as this plane contacts the ball much higher up. The part of the ball — top, middle, bottom — is very important. If you wish to strike a low ball, aim for the top half of the ball. I call it a top-the-egg shot. If you want more height, aim lower down on the ball.

Shot elevation required	The ball
High	Low contact (back-spin/steep swing)
Low	High contact (flat swing)

Fig 1.9 *If the clubhead contacts the top of the ball, it will have a very low flight.*

In the sand

You should use your feet as 'educators' when you have to play a shot from the sand. By 'shuffling' your feet you will be able to gauge for yourself the density of the sand. (See Chapter 6, Fig 6.10.) Remember, the ball will come out much faster from hard sand than from soft sand. If you feel that the sand is soft, you must play a much firmer shot, aiming to send the ball past the pin. If the sand is hard, play an easier shot.

Fig 1.10

① Eyes focusing behind ball: *This focus will help direct the swing towards the back of the ball. Also helps shoulder turn.*

② Arms hanging freely: *If you were asked to lift an object off the ground, you would move in nearly on top of it and 'lever' it up with your arms. You would never attempt to lift at full stretch.*

③ Left arm extended: *Creates wide arc to swing. Consistency comes when your left arm becomes an 'extension of the shaft'.*

④ Left shoulder tilted up: *Helps create a similar position at impact — right moves down as left moves up (an upswing hit).*

⑤ Right elbow tucked in: *Helps flat shoulder turn. Weakens the 'bully' strong right arm. Helps player get inside the ball early in the backswing.*

⑥ Weight back on right foot: *Much easier to get behind the ball.*

Closed stance: *Encourages 'in to out' swing. Swing along feet line.*

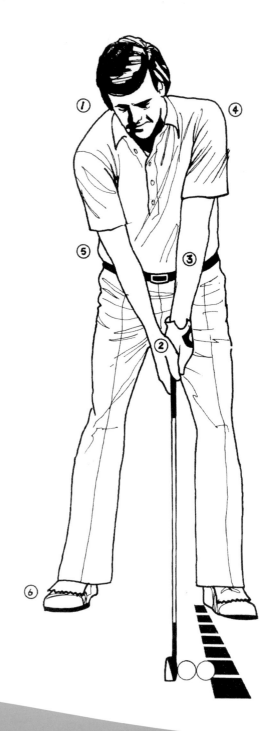

Address and impact

When you address the ball, you are making a statement. You are saying: 'This is the position I would like to be in when I strike the ball.' It is the same in every swing, good or bad. You will always tend to return to your address position at impact.

When the great players wish to alter the flight of their shots they do so by changing their address position, that is, by standing more open or more closed or.....

The point is, you may feel a fault in the hitting area which is caused by your swing, but it originated way back in your set-up. The correction is also to be found there. From setting up to impact takes approximately 1.5 seconds. If you are able to position yourself like a top-class player, you have a very good chance of returning to this position at impact.

What you do in the set-up will determine how you will be at impact, and if you wish to improve impact, you must first of all improve your position at address. As sure as night follows day, a sound set-up is followed by a good swing.

Jack Nicklaus

"If you setup correctly you will hit a reasonable shot even if you make a mediocre swing. However if you setup incorrectly you will hit the worst shot in the world even if you make the best shot."

Here is a routine you can practise at home:

Stand erect, place club in fingers of your left hand and close so that the 'V' formed by thumb and base of index finger points to right shoulder. (See Figs 1.11 and 1.12.) Extend your left arm fully. Widen stance to shoulder width. Hold your back straight up, stick your rear end out and move your weight back onto your heels. Flex your knees and hips in order to get down to the ball. Lift up your chin and turn your head to the right.

Fig 1.11 The correct way to place your left hand on the grip.

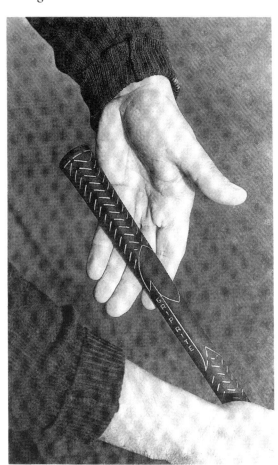

Place your right arm behind your back. Drop your right shoulder down and, using an underarm movement, place your right hand on the club so that the 'V' formed by your thumb and index finger points in the same direction as the 'V' on the left hand (towards right shoulder). Flex your right elbow inwards. This movement ensures that your stronger right arm is placed in a totally submissive position. Even though right now you may feel like an octopus, you should begin to look like the set-up shown in Fig 1.16.

Fig 1.12 Place the left hand on the grip so that the 'V' formed by the base of your index finger and thumb points in the direction of your right shoulder.

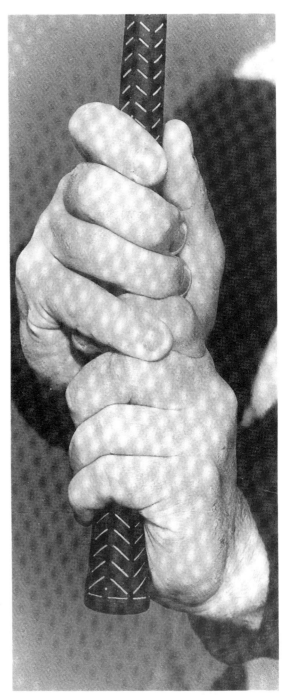

Fig 1.13 Ninety-two per cent of all professionals use this grip. It is known as the 'Vardon overlap'. Give it a try.

Practise your set-up at home

Fig 1.14 *Tuck in right elbow*
Fig 1.15 *Right arm relaxed*
Fig 1.16 *Strengthen left arm*

1.14

TUCK IN
RIGHT
ELBOW

1.16

STRENGTHEN
LEFT ARM.

1.15

RIGHT ARM RELAXED

My 'Home' Course

Longford Golf Course 'Irish golfers play in all sorts of weather'

'I would love one day to see two golf courses in Longford'

Set-up

People often ask me how I manage to change a golfer's swing, especially if his next game is at the weekend and the new swing has to work immediately! The truth is, I rarely ever have to change any player's swing. Rather, I change the set-up. I set up a whole series of different angles, angles that will guarantee a different result. In a matter of minutes I could 'set the player up' to slice, hook, sky, etc.

Any golfer who habitually slices the ball right (see Fig 1.17) will naturally fear the right-hand side and therefore aim 'away off' to the left (see Fig 1.18). This is a very human reaction. Usually when we want something to go left, for example our car, we aim to the left. The difference between the car and the golf-ball is that the car is not 'spinning' as well as moving. A golf-ball on the other hand, if it is struck left with an open clubface (pointing right), will eventually succeed in 'worming' its way to the right — every time. My advice to someone who slices the ball is this: you must attack the right-hand side of the fairway. You must change your attitude and no longer 'fear' the right — instead you must attack it. This works because golf is a game of opposites.

The golfer who hooks the ball (see Fig 1.19) will always aim away from the trouble (see Fig 1.20). I change this golfer's grip to the angle shown in Fig 1.21 and his stance to an open one (see Fig 1.18). The result: the shots begin to move in the desired direction (correcting the out-of-control hook) (see Fig 1.17).

"GOLF IS A GAME OF OPPOSITES"

1.17

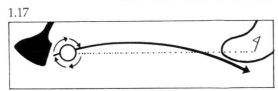

Your set-up will affect
your swing

*Fig 1.17 This shows the slice
off to the right of the green.*

1.18

*Fig 1.18 If you slice to the
right you will automatically
aim to the left in an effort
to save the shot.*

*Fig !.19 This shows the
hook off to the left of the
green.*

*Fig. 1.20 The golfer who
hooks to the left will
inevitably aim to the right.*

*Fig 1.21 To correct the
hook, change the grip angle
so that the 'V' between the
base of your index finger
and thumb points towards
your chin, and aim to the
left. This is called the 'weak
grip'.*

1.19

1.20

1.21

These changes are all made at set-up, as your grip angle controls your clubface angle at impact and your feet alignment controls your swing-line. This is why this early and rather tedious lesson is so important.

Some good advice

Set up sequential short-range goals
The secret for you now is to set up small, sequential short-range goals that are attainable, for example, instead of starting at the beginning, why not start at the end? Think of this: 65 per cent of golf is played within thirty yards (27m) of the green! We all feel (even on our worst day!) that we have the ability to strike the ball thirty yards. If we develop the technique to strike the ball accurately to the flag from thirty yards in, we will have only 35 per cent of the game left to conquer. To explain further, 43 per cent (of the 65 per cent) of the total shots you take are not on the course but on the green. In this part of the game, the ball does not actually leave the ground at all!

Count your putts
Have you ever counted your putts? If your average is three and a half putts per hole as a beginner, your total putts would amount to sixty-three. I know you can become a damn good putter — why not set yourself a simple goal? It demands absolutely no physical effort. Bring your average down to two putts per hole or thirty-six per round. If you succeed you have, in one simple move, knocked twenty-seven shots off what is considered the average score for a beginner.

Plus, think of the overall confidence it will bring to your game, and of the fear that this talent will strike into the hearts of your opponents! The great players spend 60 per cent of their practice time on their short game, the novice an average of 15 per cent! The legendary Scottish golfer Willie Park once said: 'A golfer who can putt is a match for anyone. A golfer who can't is a match for nobody!'

Observe your divots
The divot shown in Fig 1.22 indicates a swing path that is towards the left or 'out to in'. This shows that the ball is going to at least start left and will stay left or veer to the right, depending on the club you are using and the direction in which the clubface is pointing at impact.

To correct this, simply align the clubhead more to the right. Ensure that your left-hand grip is turned to the right (stronger grip). Align your feet, hips and shoulders to right. Swing along to the line of the body and make sure that you release the clubhead — do not let the body go with it.

If the divot is 'going the other way' or is straight towards the target, you are in much better shape. If the ball is still not hitting the target it is because your clubface is not pointing at the target at impact — even though you are swinging in the direction of the target. It is 'open' or 'closed'. You have to check that the face is square to where you want the ball to go.

Fig 1.22 You will inevitably play bad golf if your divots look like this. The dotted line shows the correct divot line, going in the direction of the target.

TARGET LINE

Divots orientated left of target line indicates 'out' is a bad swing

Etiquette
Respect your club's rules and the earth.

Fig 1.23 Replace divots

Fig 1.24 Repair pitch marks

Fig 1.25 Repair footprints in a bunker

'YOU DON'T MEAN...'
A friend of mine, Jack, told me an amazing story of something that happened to him. He is quite religious. He went to confession and the priest started off by saying, 'Well son, tell me your sins.'

'Bless me Father for I have sinned,' Jack confessed. 'I have used terrible language. I have taken the Lord's name in vain.' The priest said, 'Son, tell me when did this happen.' Jack replied, 'On the golf course, Father.' 'Oh, I see. I'm a keen golfer myself — maybe you would like to explain how it happened.' Jack continued, 'You see Father, I was playing in the Captain's Prize. I had a wonderful round of golf going after seventeen holes. Some of my friends came out from the clubhouse and told me that all I needed was a par to win it.'

The priest brought his head forward. He was now listening intently. 'Okay, so you knocked the ball out of bounds off the tee?' 'No, Father, that's the infuriating part,' said Jack, getting slightly irritated. 'I struck the most perfect drive, right down the middle, almost 290 yards (265m), but when I arrived, if I didn't find the ball lying over a heel mark!' 'Okay,' said Father, 'you

opening the face even more, and chopped down with the open face from the outside. The ball rose almost vertically and it dropped like a butterfly with a sore foot, fifteen inches from the hole.'

'You don't mean,' Father said heatedly, 'that you missed the ★★★★ putt!'

swore violently.' 'No, no Father! I held my composure.' (Father's head was now leaning onto the mesh separating the two of them.)

Jack went on. 'I have a beautiful 5 Wood — metal head — with a gold shaft. I visualised the ball flying like a rocket towards the green, out of the heel mark....' 'Go on.' 'Well, Father, I played the ball slightly back in my stance, took a steeper back-swing, stayed down in on the shot and played the most wonderful 5 Wood I think I ever played.'

Father was looking at him weirdly now. 'But you won't believe what happened,' said Jack. (Father was almost relieved.) 'When the ball landed, it must have struck something. If it didn't ricochet off at a terrible angle into that bunker in front of the green — you know the one I mean — the ball finished right up under the lip, an unplayable ball, Father!' 'So that's where you used the foul, abusive language,' said Father, moving back from the mesh.

'No, no, no, Father!' (Father's head lurched back again.) 'I have a sand wedge for seventeen years, a favourite old club of mine. I held my composure — visualised the perfect explosion shot. I flattened out the face of the sand wedge. I dug my feet really well into the sand. I took the club up most steeply,

CONSISTENCY IN PLAY

Golfers who decide they want to improve through tuition usually give similar answers to these questions:

Why have you come for a lesson?
What's your problem?
What would you like to work on during this half hour?

Their answers are usually some variation of: 'Well, the situation is that I can hit a great shot, even a corker, but I can never manage to repeat it consistently. I would love to be consistent.'

Do you want to know the secret of consistency?

Let's start by answering these questions:

1. *Are your shots generally too high and lack distance? Are you a short hitter?*

2. *Do you occasionally slice, pull, top, sky, shank shots?*

3. *Are you afraid to tee the ball high? Do you use a very low tee? (If so, you are protecting a bad swing.)*

4. *Are your divots going leftwards?*

5. *Are you unable to hit a 3 Iron to its full, or have you a suspect long game but an adequate short game?*

6. *Do you strike the 6 Iron and 3 Iron the same distance?*

If you answer 'Yes' to any or all of these questions, then your swing is off-plane and out of tempo (much too fast).

Consistency has to do with a slow, even tempo and a flat, wide swing-plane.

▶ TEMPO AND SWING-PLANE

Tempo and swing-plane are closely related to one another and, more importantly, to consistent shots. Think of tempo for a moment. If you drive your car slowly you may not arrive as fast as you would wish, but it is unlikely that you will have an accident on the way. In fact, if you do anything slowly you are less likely to make mistakes. The same principle applies to golf — a hurried swing will be an inconsistent one, and will give you a variety of results. A hurried swing is certain to be off-plane and much too steep — the dreaded 'V' type.

Golfers do not swing off-plane and out of tempo deliberately. They do so because of a) the mistaken idea that speed equals distance — the faster I swing, the further the ball will go (it's very hard to swing easy!), and b) the fact that our bodies contain big and small muscles. Our legs, arms and shoulders are the bigger ones, our hands and wrists the smaller ones. When we look for distance, especially with the Driver, our hands and wrists take over. High handicap golfers grip the club much too tightly — they strangle the club. You must always remember that your hands are transmitters of power — you create power in your body and transmit this power through your hands down to the clubhead at impact. A tight grip blocks this transfer.

The smaller muscles have the ability to move much faster than the arms and the shoulders — they tend to race away in the backswing. You must realise that your hands and wrists are very flexible, and capable of sudden movement. Quick sudden movements are very hard to control. Have you ever watched a great player strike the ball? Were you amazed by his/her easy tempo? The great players, from many years' experience, have learned to control their swings with the bigger muscles — the arms and shoulders. Because these muscles move much slower than the hands and wrists, they are much easier to control. These players are therefore able to consistently repeat the same swing time and again.

Quick, small muscle movements also lead to a steep, chopping swing. The simple reason why a golfer mistakenly swings too fast is because he/she is allowing the smaller muscles to take over the swing — a snatch with the hands, a quick break with the wrists. This smaller muscle movement is of course much easier to do. We prefer it. This incorrect small muscle movement will always resemble the 'V' shape, and of course be out of plane, as the quick snatch with the wrists will always prevent the 'body turn' from taking place. There is simply no time for the body to actually turn away.

Fig 2.1 Many golfers lift the club up steeply in the backswing, making a 'V' swing. This is incorrect. In order to drive the ball forwards you must learn to turn your back to the target before you lift your arms.

PLAY WITH 'DEAD HANDS'

To become consistent you must school yourself into deadening your smaller muscles — your hands and wrists — and developing a relaxed tempo by rotating the 'L' back as a unit. Turn your back on the target (see the drills at the end of this chapter). I call this the 'package deal', whereby everything turns together, with the knees resisting. This way you are on-plane with a nice easy tempo. You must learn to turn 'behind' the ball.

This 'package deal' is sometimes referred to as the 'connection theory' because the clubhead is connected to your left arm and shoulder — you should always move the shoulder, arm and clubhead as one unit.

Learn to Turn Your Back to Target

Do not break the glass

2.2 The flatter swing is best. The golfer must swing 'inside' the pane of glass.

a)

A special relationship should exist between your belly button and the top of the shaft throughout the swing. The club must never escape from the body (belly button) in the good swing. It should always be in sync with the body.

I have a saying I use during lessons: 'If you develop a flat swing, you will end up with a fat wallet. If you have a steep swing, you will always have a thin wallet!' In other words, you are on to a winner with the flat swing — the steep swing is for losers. (See Fig 2.2.)

Avoid a 'tilty' shoulder turn. School yourself into turning your shoulders at the same level. Turn your back on the target. Move your left shoulder out and right shoulder back behind you as your start your backswing. Concentrate on the shoulder plane. Your shoulders turn while your knees

2.3 This rotary drill shows the correct positions for:
a) ADDRESS — facing the ball
b) BACKSWING — turn your back to the target
c) FINISHING SWING — face to target

b)

c)

Learn to rotate during your swing

Getting great distance with your divots

resist. The reasons why you must turn are a) to set up a shallow angle whereupon you can attack the back of the ball and drive it forwards, and b) to create power. You must learn to turn your left side into your right side.

THE ROTARY SWING

Body pivot is essential for consistency. This is achieved through the rotary swing (see Fig 2.3). This works because:

1. The ball is static.
2. Your body is static.

Hammer throwers, for example, use this rotation theory whereby their shoulders rotate at right angles to their spines. Similarly, the 'body turn' plays a most important part in the golf swing. You must learn to hit the ball with your complete body, and avoid a quick swipe with your hands and wrists whilst your body remains rigid.

THE FORWARD SWING

If you thought it was difficult to sort out your backswing plane, allow me to let you in on another little secret — it is much more difficult to swing on-plane on your downswing. You must school yourself into swinging wider on your downswing than you do on your backswing. Unfortunately, most golfers swing very steep on their downswing. This is because when you swing the clubhead back it reaches a height of six feet (almost 2m) off the ground and the ball is two inches (5cm) off the ground. It has been calculated that it takes a fifth of a second for the clubhead to come from the height of six feet down to two inches, that is, from the top of the backswing to impact. When you are up in the top of your backswing, what you see (unfortunately) is the ball. For the downswing you must learn not to swing directly to the ball, rather to swing your clubhead on a shallower plane than you would on your backswing. Score a goal rather than a point (see Fig 2.4).

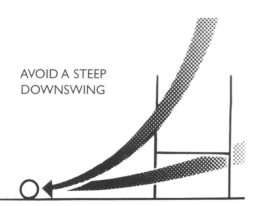

Fig 2.4 Score a goal rather than a point.

AVOID A STEEP
DOWNSWING

The better players give themselves enough time to strike the back of the ball. Good golfers 'detour' their downswings, that is, they swing the clubhead down into a shallower position first, *then* they swing it forwards. If you swing into a shallower position, the first advantage is that when the clubhead is coming in towards the back of the ball it will be travelling more or less parallel to the ground. But if you don't 'bottom out' your club, the clubhead will travel very steeply downwards at impact. The power of the swing will then go into the ground.

▶ RESIST THE POWER SYNDROME

Just before impact a thought usually comes into our minds — to give the ball a little bit more power so as to increase the pace and gain a bit extra on distance. Oscar Wilde once remarked: 'I can resist anything but temptation.' Avoid the power syndrome, no matter how tempted you may be.

If you swing wide going back, you have secured a good angle to attack the back of the ball — you must therefore take advantage of the situation you have created. If you succeed in going back low (wide), swing in on the same plane and extend your arms out after impact — in other words, repeat backswing and forward-swing planes. My message is: something good must happen on either side of the ball! Think 'wide, wide, wide'.

Force is simply a killer in the downswing. Stay 'behind' the ball. Slow down your swing effort before impact. From the top of your backswing your hands have to travel

Fig 2.5 Aggressive swings, aimed at achieving distance, are counter-productive. Here the player is hitting with the handle, resulting in an impact position in which the handle is pointing forwards and the clubhead is lagging behind — an inevitable slice.

THE BLOCK SWING

approximately three feet (1m) in order for them to reach level with the ball, while the clubhead has to travel approximately nine feet (3m). Therefore your hands have to travel one third of the distance of the clubhead. The clubhead is on the outer extremity and the hands are on the inner extremity. If you decide to apply a little

Fig 2.6 Wait for the clubhead to catch up with your hands. Diagram shows the short distance the hands have to travel compared to the clubhead.

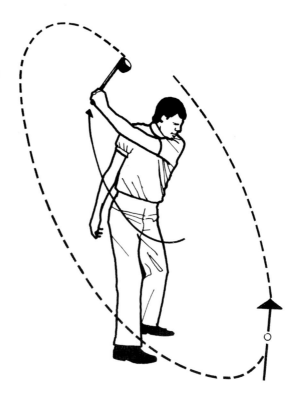

more force and move your body forward, your hands will automatically move faster through the impact area, so the clubhead will lag even further behind. The clubhead will also come down very steeply on the ball.

You must activate the clubhead. It is very important to keep on your own side of the 'road' — not to swing down and across, rather to swing down on the inside and thereafter out through the ball — from inside out. Get the feeling of swinging the club on-plane from the top of the backswing in towards the back of the ball. If you want to be a good golfer, you must allow your club to go down and out. Stay 'inside' before impact.

AVOID THE 'BAD' SHOTS

There are only nine possible bad shots in
golf. If you swing from outside, you will
make an 'out to in' swing, and this may
result in any or all of the following six bad
shots.

If you swing off-plane on your downswing
(that is, steep), you will be swinging at the
ball from outside and across the swing-line.
The most likely result of this is the *slice shot*
— the clubhead will be coming from out to
in and will be slightly open to the swing-line.
This is a problem for 75 per cent of golfers.

Then there is the *pull shot* where the
clubface is square to the swing-line and the
ball goes straight to the left.

As the clubhead is descending very sharply it
is possible that you may actually come down
on 'top' of the ball — this is called a *top
shot*.

As the clubhead is coming off-plane, down
towards the ball, it is also possible that you
may hit the bottom of the ball and 'sky' it
into the air — a *sky shot*.

Because the clubhead is coming down very
steeply, it may 'fluff' into the ground — this
is referred to as a *fluff shot*.

With the Iron shot, especially up around the
green, if you swing outside on the
downswing, the clubhead may not make
contact with the ball at all. It will be the
'shank' of the club that will hit the ball — a
so-called *shank shot*.

Fig 2.7 Be aware of the results of an incorrect swing-line: a) shows 'out to in' swing-line; b) shows resulting bad shots; c) shows 'in to out' swing-line; d) shows resulting good shots.

Some people like to swing a little bit off-plane on their backswings, but you must learn to swing on-plane as you come into the ball. The common denominator of every great player is that they are right at impact, irrespective of how they get there, and every

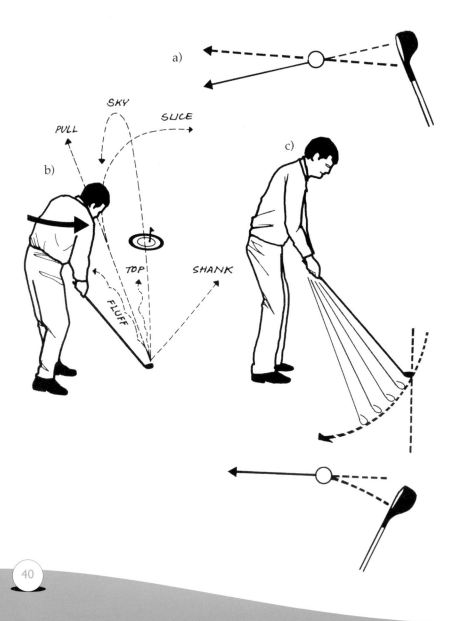

one of them hits the ball from the *inside*.
They arrive into a position where the
clubhead is coming in on a shallow plane,
where the right elbow is brushing off their
side (right hip). If you can learn to get into
this area on your downswing, you will have
eliminated 75 per cent of the bad shots.

Let me tell you a secret of golf, a way in
which it is nearly impossible to hit a bad
shot: you must start by deadening the
muscles in your hands and wrists and
schooling yourself to swing on-plane, turning
the 'L', starting your forward swing by
rotating your left hip out of the way, thus

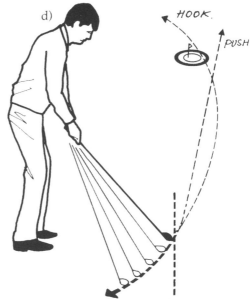

creating clubhead speed, and then
approaching from the inside towards the
back of the ball, extending your arms out
after impact. In other words, you have to
work your bigger muscles to swing them on-
plane and try to swing on a shallower plane
on the downswing than on the backswing.

▶ SWING TIPS

Turn flat on your backswing but don't swing flat as you follow through. From my experience, the most common mistakes that practising golfers make are: a) failure to turn their shoulders in the backswing (to get 'inside', to get an angle on the ball), b) swinging down and across the line through impact.

Let there be absolutely no doubt about it — swinging across the line is the biggest fault in the game. You must remember the following (an amazing piece of information you might say!): your arms are attached to your shoulders! So much so that they do not like going away from them. I cringe when I see the swings of so many potentially good players collapsing leftwards at impact. When I say 'turn flat — don't swing flat', what I

Fig 2.8 Right elbow to right hip is the first move on the downswing. This results in the correct 'inside' position.

mean is that the most important part of the swing happens AFTER you strike the golf-ball. You must school yourself into swinging wide on your follow-through. Force your arms out after impact, extend the triangle down the line and stop halfway into your follow-through. Check your left arm — has it collapsed too early? I am not suggesting you finish your full swing with your two arms in a fully extended position. I am saying, widen

your follow-through before you relax your
arms at the end. Lock it to the target.

Another tip — once you have pin-pointed
your target, forget about where it actually is.
While in the practice area look at another
(imaginary) target — well right of the real
one. Lock your follow-through 'out' to this
one. It's an 'optical illusion' you must
perform. Swing right of where you want the
ball to go. Because your arms are attached
to your shoulders, if you don't do this
'imaginary' right swing, you will find yourself
swinging left of the target.

*Fig 2.9 To achieve
consistency you must learn
to extend your arms
outwards after impact. Swing
to the right, to an
imaginary target. This will
result in a wide follow-
through.*

IMAGINARY TARGET

I often think that hitting a drive off a tee is like taking the ball on the fly! Imagine that the ball has been tossed to you and you must take it on the fly before it hits the ground. Think of the sweeping swing you would use. In the same way, you must learn to sweep the ball away off the tee.

Fig 2.10 Don't force the feel, feel the force.

'SMILE' AT IMPACT

▶ THE IMPORTANCE OF T-E-M-P-O

Rotate in tempo: It is very hard to swing 'easy'!

I remember giving a lesson to a player who had a steep swing that was also quick and jerky. He was demanding distance as a right and was very inconsistent. I jokingly said to him: 'Do you know you are supposed to smile as you strike, not grimace.' I also said: 'Imagine your nick-name is S-M-O-O-T-H-I-E, that you have a smooth swing, and just think of driving the ball a short distance.' His tempo and plane improved dramatically, as did his consistency. Have the confidence to hit the ball softly.

Learn to use an 8 Iron tempo with your Driver. Don't look for distance. Let it come to you. As the saying goes, 'Don't force the feel', rather 'feel the force'. Allow your tempo and an accurate strike to do the job. I often compare a golf swing with driving a pin into wood with a hammer. The pin is so delicate — if you strike it too hard, you will bend it. You must give it just the right amount — an accurate strike with an even tempo.

Remember, the golf swing is one continuous motion, a repeating rotating swing, respecting angles and pace.

Fig 2.11 In order to achieve maximum distance with minimum effort you must learn to hit the ball with your Driver only on the upswing.

SWING "UP" THROUGH

▶ DRILLS

Practice routine 1
Power posture
1. Squat
2. Stick out your rear end

Practise hitting 'soft' shots with a half-swing. Widen the middle of your swing. Get rid of the 'V' swing forever.

Power creation
3. Transfer and turn your upper body against the resistance of your knees — the foundation of the swing. (See Fig 2.12(b).)

Power release on shallow plane
4. Rotate the left hip. (See Fig 2.12(c).)
5. Finish with the middle of your belt facing the target.
6. Extend your two arms out after impact ('Package deal').

Use rotation to help create clubhead speed. Use an 8 Iron and tee a dozen balls in a row. Practise 'pushing' the ball forwards eighty yards (75m) using the half-swing, finishing with arms fully extended in the triangle position.

Practise the above drills as often as you can, with or without a club. The famous American instructor Gene O'Brien once said: 'I shall always stress that it is quite easy to hit a golf-ball consistently after you have taught yourself how to swing a golf club away from the ball.'

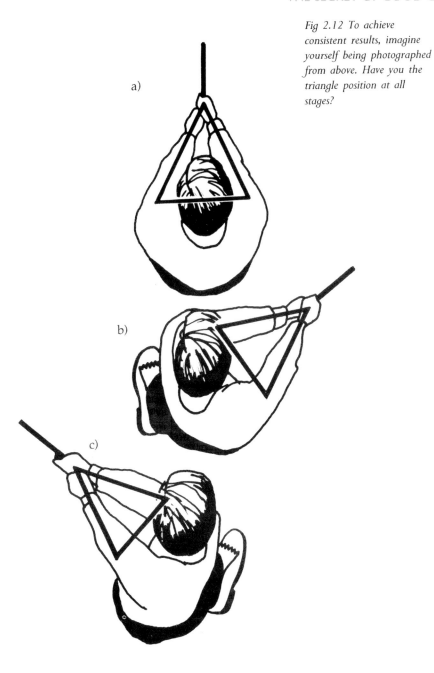

Fig 2.12 To achieve consistent results, imagine yourself being photographed from above. Have you the triangle position at all stages?

Keep saying the following to yourself as you practise your swing:

'I am standing above.'
'I must turn behind (back to target).'
'Hit the back of the ball.'
'Move through (clear left side).'
'Finish with my arms in the triangle position.'

Fig 2.13 If you hit the ball on the upswing, you will get a clean hit and maximum distance.

Practice routine 2

Do the following drill:

- Develop a swing with a forward momentum.
- Flatten the middle of your swing. (See Fig 1.6.)
- Place one golf-ball on the ground, another ball on the tee. (See Fig 2.13.)
- Sweep clubhead over the ball on the tee at full speed.
- Memorise that 'feel' and use it while striking.
- Learn to sweep the clubhead up as you strike.

I call this the 'Hit it up to heaven' drill. The secret of drive is to 'nearly' top the ball. Remember, there is no bottom to the good swing. You are at an unfortunate angle at address. You are standing above the ball. Normally when you wish to move anything forwards, you place your body behind that object.

Fig 2.14 Don't make the ball the focal point of your swing. It must be incidental to your swing.

SUMMARY

The big thing in golf is to move behind the ball on the backswing and hold the shallow angle through the swing — don't give it away. The secret is to recognise a bad angle at address and to do something about it. Create an angle of attack where you can strike the back of the ball.

I often feel that the ball occupies a huge place in the beginner's mind. The whole swing, every sinew, all thoughts, are centred around getting that ball away. Doubts exist as to whether the club will contact it, hit it a distance, slice it or not. It is as if there is a brick wall just behind the ball and a great effort is made right up to impact, but the swing suddenly collides with the wall and stops right there. No follow-through.

SUFFERING FROM "BALLITIS"

In the better players' swing, the body tension and anxiety is not as dominant. The distance hit is not as crucial. Good players swing 'past' the ball, as if it was not there — sweep through it smoothly. They avoid hitting at the ball — they move through it. I remember watching Ian Woosnam hit shots at our driving range one day. The thing that struck me was the way he moved through the ball.

49

His left hip cleared beautifully every time. His body moved with the swing. There was no sensation of 'hit'. So the message is: 'Don't make the ball the focal point of your swing!'

Fig 2.15 Clearing the left side a) Backswing b) Impact c) Finish
Good rotation of the hips will allow complete follow-through.

You know when you have struck the ball well the moment after impact. You know that 'feeling', without ever having to look up. It feels almost as if you struck nothing,

a)

b)

as if there was no 'resistance' at impact. It's a wonderful feeling. The knack is to swing wide. So, do not make the ball the focal point of your *next* swing. Swing past it. Forget about your backswing. Give it a big follow-through.

Remember: The most important part of the swing happens after impact.

Fig 2.16 At impact, bad golfers will have their left hip facing the ball, while good golfers will have their mid-line facing the target.

c)

ST PETERSBURG

A golfer got to heaven and found it was full of great golf courses. One of them looked really tough. He was watching a golfer trying to strike a ball over an enormous lake onto a green 350 yards away.

'Who does he think he is — Jesus Christ?' asked the newcomer.

'That is Jesus Christ,' said a passing angel. 'His trouble is, he thinks he's Seve Ballesteros.'

CHOOSING THE CORRECT 'ANGLES'

A question! What is the most important thing in golf, and why? The answer — the angle of the clubface precisely as it strikes the ball at impact. A fact — it does not matter in which direction you swing in golf! If you swing left and your clubface is facing right (open to the swing-line), the ball will never end up left of target — it will always slice off to the right. It is not the direction that is important, but what angle your clubface is at as it collides with the static ball. I often tell pupils: 'The important thing is how you arrive, not how you drive!'

Fig 3.1 If you want the ball to travel towards the target, the clubface must be square as it strikes the ball.

▶ SHAPING YOUR SHOT

If you think golf is a difficult game, you will be convinced after this chapter! The real problem is that you can strike a ball in a certain direction but it may well not have the decency to stay there! Take for example the dreaded slice shot, where the ball finishes way right of the target (see Fig 3.2). This shot actually starts off left of the target. I often compare what happens in this shot to a boat going down a river. Your arms are like the power, the engine and the body of the boat. The rudder is the clubface. The smallest change in the angle of the rudder will have a huge bearing on the direction of the boat. Amazingly, the slightest change in the clubface angle at impact has a huge bearing on the flight of the ball. Unfortunately you will never witness this at impact as it happens so fast — too fast for the eye to behold. You will only see the resulting shot.

Fig 3.2 This open clubface will result in a slice.

The slice is probably the most common 'bad' shot in golf. It is always most frustrating. All that effort for a high, weak shot. I am always reminded of someone pouring water into a bucket with a big hole in it. The water (power) is escaping. The cause is an open clubface. The cure is to 'knuckle down' — show more knuckles on your left hand grip — the finger grip (see Fig 1.11). This may feel terribly uncomfortable at first but the result, if you are able to put up with it, will be dramatic because with this alteration in your grip you will present a closed position at impact. The balls will tend to go straight, or you may even hook them slightly to the left. So you must change your 'attitude' and stop anticipating the slice to the right. Attack the area where you are having the problem — go straight for it. Aim right if you are afraid of the right, do not anticipate the slice. If you succeed in swinging it out to the right, you have cured both your clubface angle and swing-line problems. Remember, it only works because of the awkwardness!

EXAGGERATE THE CURE

I will let you in on a trade secret: when afflicted with the open (or closed for that matter) clubface at impact, never try to move directly to the square position. Always try to exaggerate the cure. Go from open to trying to close the face. If you are lucky, the clubface will return square at impact. I always say there is some excuse for hitting a different type of bad shot in golf, but there is no excuse for striking the same old tired slice or hook shot again and again. If you cannot shape your shots, you haven't got what I call 'a handle on the game'. You do not understand the importance of your clubface angles as you address the ball, throughout the entire swing and most especially at impact. Your clubface angle at impact determines how you play!

Golf is all about ball control. A good tip is to hold the clubface angle square to the flag as you strike the ball. This works even on putts — hold the putter head square to the hole as you strike the putt, marry one to the other.

(See the typical 'golf lesson' on correcting the slice in the Appendix: Lesson 1.)

▶ THE ANGLES

There are three angles the clubface can take at impact: square, open, and closed (see Figs 3.3, 3.4, 3.5). The clubface can hold one of these three positions throughout the entire swing.

| *Fig 3.3 Square clubface* | *Fig 3.4 Open clubface* | *Fig 3.5 Closed clubface* |

SLICE   HOOK

If a golfer presents the *closed* clubface at the top of his backswing, I know immediately that he will hook or pull left, and the ball will end up left of the target. His shots will lack height and he will have desperate trouble chipping around the green. His Driver will also be rested for some time! (The Driver face has an 11 degree loft: if even slightly closed at impact the ball will never get airborne.) These type of shots have a lot of top-spin on them when the ball hits the ground and they generally create more distance.

If you strike with an *open* clubface (the clubface pointing right of the target), the ball will end up right of target. Shots with an open clubface will also be very high and lack distance. Much of the force of your swing is lost through the open clubface. The open clubhead creates back-spin so that the shots lack distance and tend to kick sideways on landing.

If you strike the ball with the clubface *squarely* on target, your shot will be on target.

Generally speaking, golfers who play with the closed face are very bad players around the green. Their short game is appalling while their long game may be adequate. When a golfer says: 'I have a good long game but a poor short game', I suspect that a closed clubface at impact is responsible. Alternatively, if he/she suffers from a poor long game and a good short game, the problem is an open face at impact.

Fig 3.6 If the hands are positioned as shown, it will inevitably lead to a closed clubface at impact.

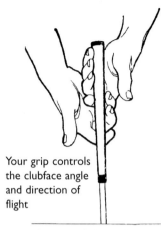

Your grip controls the clubface angle and direction of flight

A strong 3 knuckle grip

This grip angle will prevent a slice and increase your distance

THE GRIP GAUGE

A tense grip is a disaster in golf!

What you do at one end of the club has a huge bearing on the other end. Your grip has a huge bearing on the clubface angle. Amazingly, golfers who slice and hook the ball are always trying to correct the fault by swing alterations. They may feel a fault in the strike and may well hit a very bad shot. While this is caused in part by a bad swing, the faulty impact originated further back than the swing — it was in the actual grip. Top-class players always change the flight pattern by altering the grip position, rarely ever changing their swing. The altered grip position effects the flight changes for them. Bad golf/good golf — flight changes start in the grip.

You must learn to operate the 'grip gauge'. Here's how it works. Your hands and arms have a natural, neutral position (a set angle) when they are hanging from the body. Once you move your hands out of this natural, normal position, they will want to revert immediately back to normality (to the original angle).

Strong grip

For example, if I place my two hands as shown in Fig 3.6 they will feel uncomfortable, and the very first chance they get they will revert back to the neutral position (try this out for yourself). In other words during the backswing they will turn back towards normality and so close the clubface, thus presenting a closed position at impact (see Fig 3.5). The ball will definitely lack height and will go leftwards. Short-game problems are a certainty. I call this right-hand position 'fisting it' — right hand grip is in the palm and much too tight.

Weak grip

Similarly, if I position my left hand as shown in Fig 3.7 during the swing, it rotates back and opens the face, resulting in the inevitable slice (see Fig 3.2). I will always remember a 'knowledgeable' man who told me he had a hook problem for twenty years. He was forever trying to correct his swing.

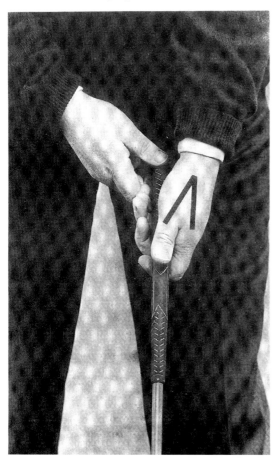

Fig 3.7 The 'V' on the left hand, pointing towards the left shoulder, signifies a weak grip and a resulting open clubface and sliced shut right.

He felt it too humiliating to admit that the actual problem was in his grip! I must make one very important point here: there is no such thing as *the* perfect grip (there is, however, such a thing as a bad grip), but there is *one* perfect grip for you. I call this the 'grip gauge'. Your barometer must be the flight of the ball on your shots.

▶ SQUARE AT IMPACT PLEASE!

An amazing fact is that the clubface only needs to be square *precisely as it hits the ball*. Many golfers are under two misconceptions, the first being that you must swing the club straight back and straight through. This is actually impossible because what results is a steep swing. As your arms are attached to your shoulders, if you try to swing straight back, the club will inevitably go outside, very steep, and you will always come 'across' the ball. The second misconception is that you must hold the clubface square for the duration of the swing. This is another impossibility and has disastrous consequences. What happens? The clubface closes on the backswing and is very closed at impact — shots hook, or even pull-hook, left.

So what happens in the actual golf swing? The clubface is square as you start. What you hope for is that you will return to square at impact, but by turning the body, the 'L' turn, the clubface is in the half-way position. This appears to be an open position, but the clubface is actually square to the body. As you will see in Fig 3.10, at the top of the backswing the clubface can be in three positions: a closed position (A) whereby shots will be left and lacking height; an open position (B) which will result in a slice, and the square position — the correct angle (C).

3.8

3.9

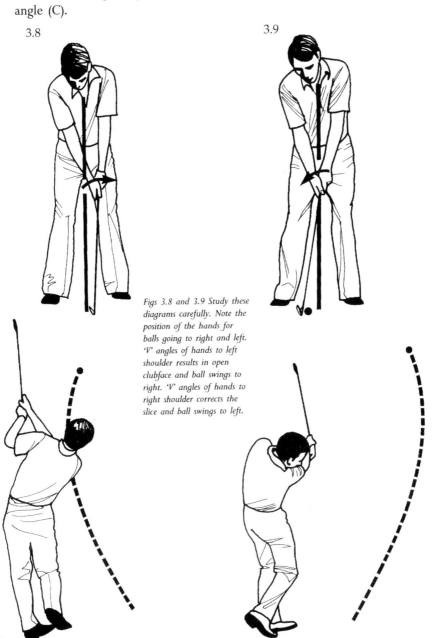

Figs 3.8 and 3.9 Study these diagrams carefully. Note the position of the hands for balls going to right and left. 'V' angles of hands to left shoulder results in open clubface and ball swings to right. 'V' angles of hands to right shoulder corrects the slice and ball swings to left.

Fig 3.10 Clubface angles at top of backswing will determine the impact positions.

a) Shut clubface — a certain hook

b) Open clubface — a sure slice

c) Square at top — correct angle

IT'S A MARRIAGE!

If the clubface is open to the swing-line, or closed, you are going to get swerve on the shot, and this could result in a pull to the left or a push to the right. If you can get the direction of your swing towards the target and your clubface square to that, all will go on line.

▶ SUMMARY

'Slice right — knuckle down'

If your shots are 'high' and 'right', you should position your hands more to the right of the grip. As you move your hands away from their normal position, they will work their way back during the swing and present a slightly closed face at impact. (See Fig 3.9.)

'Leftward shots — Hooks — No knuckles'

If your shots are flying 'left' and 'low', operate the grip gauge in a different manner. Move your hands to the left. Weaken your grip. Your hands will tend to work their way back to normality and open out the clubface at impact. (See Fig 3.8.)

You must have the determination and concentration to work on your grip — find a grip gauge angle that works for *you*.

a)

CLOSED CLUBFACE ON TOP

b)

OPEN

c)

SQUARE

A GRIPPING STORY!

John McDermott had the worst slice in the club. One day he surpassed himself with his slice. The golf course ran anti-clockwise (traditional) and all the trouble was on the right-hand side — the slicer's nightmare. He sliced the fifth tee off, sixth, seventh, eighth. At the ninth he teed up the ball and aimed away to the left in order to prevent the shot going right. He struck the ball very hard and it sailed right over the wall on the right-hand side, hit a car windscreen and shattered it. The car collided with a van, almost killing the unfortunate driver. After giving details to the police, John carried on. Having lost nine more golf-balls, he headed for the eighteenth hole. He shot the ball right through the professional's shop window! Both the secretary and the professional stormed over to John. 'What are you going to do about it?' screamed the professional. 'I think,' said John, 'if I move my left hand a little more over the shaft....'

"RELEASE THE CLUBHEAD"

*You should look on your **wrists** as your **engine** as this is where the **power** is going to come from, it is in the **wrists**.*

CAR ENGINE

*You **release** the **head** to the **ball** with your wrists.*

Diagram 86

Your Wrists are Your Engine
The hitting area where all the top players are the same!

I am often asked what is the most important thing in the game from the teaching point of view, or if I was given five minutes what would I choose to talk on, or alternatively is there one thing above everything else that is most important in the game. *(See diagram 86)*

I always come back to one point. It is this, that you have to learn to hit the ball first and control it later. Most of the established tour players have already conquered the first aspect and are seeking to refine the other. Hence, their coaching is based around this control concept, most of the time. On the other hand the majority of potentially good players who come to me for tuition are seeking the first — to hit the ball a maximum distance with less effort. The problem arises from their natural interest in improving and that this actually works against them, for they, generally speaking, read up on any material they feel might help them. This advice is written by tour professionals whom the magazine owners feel will sell copies for them (who wants to read an unknown!). The distance factor does not enter this class of player's theorising. It is also true to say that they are at their physical peak and at the top of their professions.

All this leads up to the fact that there is a huge gulf between the tour professional and the potentially good player, and even more between the tour professional and the novice. He can have no idea of how little the novice knows, or how he actually feels when for example he stands on the first tee and wonders is he going to hit it right, left, sky, top or even hit a corker. To quote Henry Longhurst, "I sometimes wonder whether the likes of me — I will not say us — can really be helped by the likes of Jack Nicklaus. He cannot have any conception, fortunately enough of what it feels to be like me. Tuck a pillow in front of his trousers, enfeeble his left eye, drain three quarters of his strength from his hands and fingers, make him pant when walking up slopes and cause the blood to rush to his head if the ball falls off the tee and he has to bend down to pick it up again, then he might begin to get the idea." It is hard for the tour player to comprehend the situation where every shot is a ''one-off situation''. Now I know we all have ''inflated'' ideas about our game that is why it is said that ''golf is the greatest game of all to play badly''. Your partner in a four-ball could after a few ''sweetners'' at the bar start to describe some of his more classical strokes, to the extent you might begin to wonder if you were in the same four-ball as him at all or if he was talking about someone else! To quote Tommy Armour, the legendary Scottish golfer, ''the expert player manages to hit between six or eight good shots in every round, the rest are good misses.......''

We manage to disguise it through the handicap system (when have you last heard a club player talk of his gross score, he always refers to the nett). The problem relates to the fact that the vast majority do not come to the game until they have reached their late twenties, early thirties or even later. The tour player on the other hand, is in his twenties, at the peak of his fitness, and generally wants 'width' in his swing with a good 'extension' through the ball — to keep it on line. This body teaching works very badly for the potentially good player because, first of all he does not have the physical fitness, the strength, the flexibility and the agility or the engine of the other. In fact many times he is a successful businessman who in his quest for sucess in the business world neglected his physical fitness. His whole life is conditioned towards success so he now proceeds to attack golf like he did his job. With the untrained and neglected body which is the price he has paid for his long struggle for success he attempts to play like the top tour players!

The net result is that the potentially good player misinterprets what is written and is off on a useless tangent.

Delegate the clubhead to work for you

''The engine or power part of your body are your wrists''. It boils down to one thing, the potentially good player, once he has organised himself for the shot should forget the body talk, and turn away on the back swing, but when he is hitting the ball realise that **his engine or the power part of his body are his wrists. That is where he is going to get his power from.** In many cases, the theorising from still photos cause him to come upon the idea that he must hold his wrists still when he is hitting the ball or, to lead with the left all the way. *(See diagrams 88 & 89).*

The most important thing in the game is to use the wrists when striking the ball. If he doesn't what happens is that the clubhead and your arms are travelling at the same speed through the ball. This results in a lack of distance and no control. The ability to "crack the whip", "skip the stone over the water" (using an underhand movement) or give the clubhead a swish with your wrists is the most important. Suddenly the ball begins to "fly" with no effort. *(See diagram 90).*

Don't force the feel, feel the force of the clubhead "Swing slow but let the clubhead go!"

There are a few pitfalls, however. **Don't confuse fast hands with a fast swing.** They are completely different. You could be swinging very fast and the clubhead not be moving nearly so fast. If you want to really move the ball you will have to move the clubhead and it is your wrists that will move it for you. **The secret is in the wrists.**

Another pitfall is to try the routine with the "big sticks" on the full shots, like a lot of things in life you have to "sneak up on it". Try doing it this way. Take an eight iron and practise chipping the ball using a **short-back-swing.** Be careful not to roll the wrists on the take away. Keep everything quiet going back — not too slow, in tempo. Do not speed up coming into the ball, just use your wrists to propel the ball forward, give it a flick with your wrists like tossing a line out to fish.

Are you a Shudda player?

I "SHUDDA" HAD A 63

You can work hard or . . .

This is the most comon fauli in golf – moving body into the ball trying to **muscle it.**

THE BACK BLOCK SWING

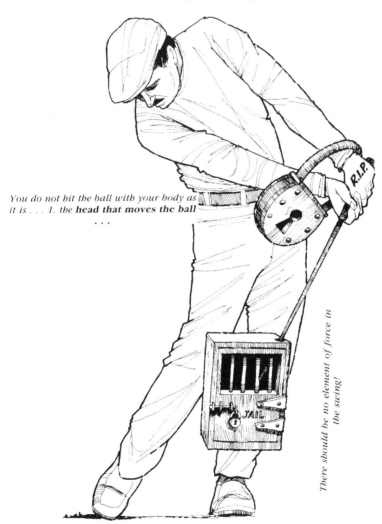

You do not hit the ball with your body as it is . . . 1. the **head that moves the ball . . .**

There should be no element of force in the swing!

Diagram 88 **CLUBHEAD HELD BACK (IN JAIL)**

. . .you can work smart

If only you could do this – keep your top half back and release the clubhead with your right hand at the ball.

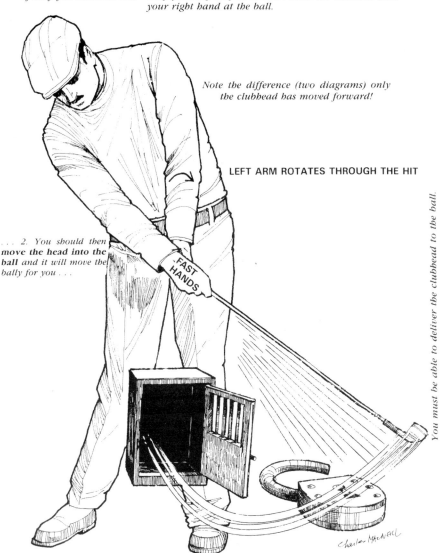

Note the difference (two diagrams) only the clubhead has moved forward!

LEFT ARM ROTATES THROUGH THE HIT

. . . 2. You should then **move the head into the ball** *and it will move the bally for you . . .*

You must be able to deliver the clubhead to the ball.

Let the head of the club to at the ball.

Diagram 89 "**CLUBHEAD RELEASED**"

Don't look for distance and for the first time in your life, **"feel the power of the clubhead"**. Think clubhead.

When you have experienced it with one club you can use it with them all. Practise with the easy ones, then you will have eliminated one problem — hitting the ball with a difficult club. You are then able to concentrate on working **"release the clubhead with your wrists"** into your game. Use this with all clubs — look at the face of the driver look at the name on the head what ever it may be, Lee Trevino, Jack Nicklaus — take a motto "make Jack do the work", give him a swish with your wrists and once again not a fast swing — final motto **"swing slow but let the clubhead go"**.

Ways to Practise Release of the Clubhead

1. One way is by turning the club upside down and gripping the club by the head. While you are swinging try to make a 'whipping' noise with the shaft through the hitting area. If the shaft is only moving at the same speed as your arms there will not be any whipping noise.

"Flick clubhead with your right wrist"

2. Practise placing the clubhead in heavy grass, then make a normal swing but practice swinging the clubhead through the heavy grass. The golfer with the best hand action in the world is undoubtedly Severiano Ballesteros. It is interesting to note that he was not allowed to practise on the fairways as a young man. He had to practise in the rough and so developed great hand action. If you are on the fairway and want to impersonate the feel, imagine you are in heavy rough and are trying to whip the ball out off the shaft. Develop the mentality that is somebody were to put their hand in to stop the clubhead, you would whip the hand off them.

3. Put a stone on the end of a piece of string and practise swinging, in the same way as you feel the stone at the end of the string you should try to feel the clubhead at the end of the shaft. *(See diagrams 90 & 90a)*.

4. A fourth way is to look on it like you were hammering a nail into a piece of timber. You would not swing your whole body at the nail, instead you would use a wrist action to release the head of the hammer at the nail. An even better example is splitting a log with an axe. You have to let the head of the axe do the splitting for you in the same way as the clubhead moves the ball. Look on the clubhead like the head of the axe, feel that just as you swing the head of the axe at the piece of timber you are swinging the clubhead at the ball.

5. A fifth way of practising the release of the wrists is to look on it as

*Use your **strong hand** when striking in under to prevent a slice, and obtain your maximum distance.*

Diagram 90 **REPEAT THIS ACTION WHEN STRIKING THE BALL**

if the hands are the centre-point. Imagine that they are not moving laterally but only the wrists and the clubhead are. It is like pulling elastic and then letting it go, but not going with it. 'Separation'. ''Free the clubhead from your body swing''. Releasing the clubhead means freeing the clubhead in your swing from your body swing. In other words you do not go with the clubhead through the hitting area but you let the clubhead go. Remember the locked swing is one where there is no wrist cock and body moves into hitting area leaving clubhead behind. Releasing the clubhead starts by realising that it is the clubhead and not yourself that moves the ball, and becoming aware of it. In the swing start by waggling the clubhead, and make certain of the wrist cock on the backswing and on downswing just let clubhead go. (Try this drill. Get a piece of elastic, stretch it between your hands and let it go from your right hand, it will immediately smack off your left hand. Now stretch it again and as you release the elastic from your right hand let the hand go with it. The speed with which it smacks off your left hand is greatly reduced. It is the same with the clubhead, you either let it off (release it) or go with it and so reduce clubhead speed *(See diagram 91)*.

A way of practising this while you are in a sitting position, is place your arms along your knees and practise moving your right hand over your left at speed without moving your arms. This position prevents you from moving your arms. Unfortunately if somebody mentions releasing the wrists the golfer tends just to speed up his swing, and get even more ahead of the ball at impact. It is not until he realises that a fast clubhead has very little or nothing to do with a fast swing that he or she understands what releasing the wrists really means.

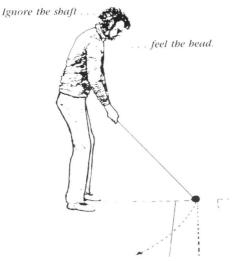

Ignore the shaft . . .

. . . feel the head.

Diagram 90a   *. . . and swing it at the ball from the inside.*

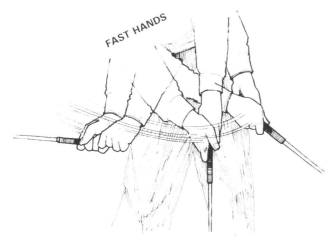

FAST HANDS

Diagram 91 Fast hands (not a fast swing) creates clubhead speed and distance.

► SUMMARY

I have talked about the slow tempo of the great players, yet the enormous distances they manage to drive the ball — I call this the 'slow fast swing' or 'stiff wristy swing'. Slow body swing — fast clubhead. It reminds me of the perfect swimmer, the duck — so graceful, gliding along over the water, hardly causing a ripple. Nothing much seems to be happening, yet the webbed feet are very active under the water. It is the same in the good golf swing — the great players are very discreet with their power. Their upper body remains very steady at impact (economy of movement), but they are working the

Backswing is "upstairs"

Downswing is "downstairs"

Fig 4.10 Turn your top half on your backswing, during the downswing move the lower half of your body and release the clubhead.

clubhead very hard. When you notice them grimace at impact, you must understand that they are trying very hard to hold their body in position (back) while they bend the clubhead end on the ball. The slow body and the activated clubhead. The clubhead, like

the webbed feet, is the accelerator of the
ball — and they know it!

We all have basic power. We can lift a
chair, push a car, chop a log. Can we use
this power in golf? Power is created by
turning the top half against the resisting
lower half going back, and by the wrist cock,
and resisting the impulse to lunge forward
on the forward swing, rather to release the
lower half and the clubhead. Think of an
elevator — the power is stored on the
second floor of your backswing. However,
you must drop it all down to the first floor
if you are to benefit from it at impact. Most
golfers spend their time fooling around on
the wrong floor! They lunge their upper
body forward at impact and hit with the
handle of the club. It's upstairs going back
and downstairs on the forward swing.

**'Distance' through
'Resistance'**

SON OF A ....

Father Murphy, the new curate, was encouraged to join the local golf club. He was a terrible golfer. Members quickly found out and avoided him.

One Saturday he was lucky enough to find a new member who agreed to play with him. The newcomer suggested they put a decent wager on the game. The priest fancied his chances as the newcomer scraped the first hole.

Once the money went on, however, all changed. Suddenly the newcomer played like a man possessed. He beat Fr Murphy and won the five pounds wager.

'Tell me,' said Fr Murphy, 'do your parents live in the parish?'

'Yes,' replied the newcomer, slightly puzzled. 'Why, would you like to meet them for a game?'

'No,' said Fr Murphy, 'a thought occurred to me. If you brought them round to the church one day, I'd marry them!'

READING BALL FLIGHT

GETTING A 'HANDLE' ON YOUR GAME

Have you ever wondered why one day you play well and think you have it, then you go out the next day and play the most awful golf? Or you play a storming front nine and then your game collapses. Why? Simply because you do not have a handle on the game. When you are on your own the teaching pro is the golf ball. It never lies. The ball in the air draws a picture of your swing on the ground. A teaching pro I once knew used to insist on turning his back on his pupils, observing only the ball flight and taking the directions solely from it. I have always thought there is some excuse for striking a different type of bad shot, but none for repeating the same one. Your attitude must be to never ever say 'What did I do wrong in the swing?', rather to ask 'What does the little ball tell me?' The reason this is important is because golf is a game of opposites. Ben Hogan once remarked: 'If you do the opposite to every natural instinct you have, you will come near the perfect swing.' There is nothing logical about golf and we are instinctively set up wrong for it. When things begin to go wrong with our shots, we become frustrated and end up taking all the wrong options. For example, if you swing leftwards the ball will most likely go to the right. And in order to save the shot you will try to hit the ball even more to the left. This will of course have the opposite effect. Similarly, if you swing down on the ball, the most likely

"Avoid practising mistakes!"

result will be the 'sky' shot. If you swing very hard and force the shot, you will put all the force into the handle of the club and probably lose distance, as no power is getting down to the clubhead.

BALL FLIGHT

The earliest golf-balls were made from wood. There was a major breakthrough in 1848 with the gutta percha ball, which was filled with a rubber-like substance. Initially this had a smooth surface and tended to go up and come down very quickly. It was found that after some time — when it became damaged through use — the ball began to hang in the air for longer, and thus the idea of markings on the face of the ball (indentations) came

Fig 5.1 You must learn to 'read' the ball flight if you want to correct your game.

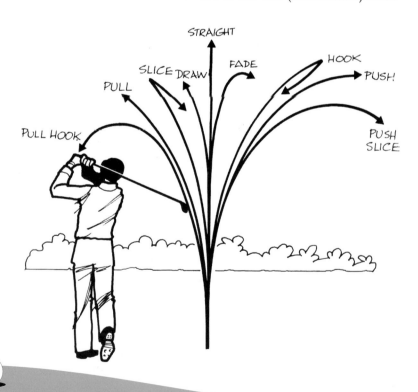

about. The modern ball with its dimple effect stays airborne for much longer. However, with this added advantage comes serious problems.

Spin and swerve

Consider the flight of a golf shot from beginning to end: a) the ball can start out in the direction of the target, or left or right of it, b) it can go very high, reasonably high, or low, c) it can swerve left or right at the end of the flight, or it can hit the target. The direction the ball takes off in is a result of what is called the *swing-line*, the direction your arms are going in, and the force of the shot will dominate the early part of the flight. Now, as the force begins to die off, whatever direction that golf-ball is spinning in (this is the result of the *clubface angle* at impact), that is going to be the major factor. The point here is very simple. You may well swing left but the clubface angle could be pointing right at impact, so that even though you may drive the ball leftwards, it might be 'spinning' towards the right. As the force begins to die, the spin takes over. In the slice shot, probably the most common shot in golf, the ball starts out to the left and wickedly veers to the right towards the end.

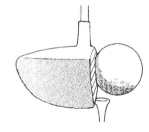

What has happened here is that the golfer has swung across the ball to the left with an open clubface. He has driven the ball leftwards and, even though it initially travels leftwards, it is spinning towards the right and will, as the force begins to die away, veer round towards the right at the end of the flight. To repeat what has happened: his arms have swung leftwards, but his clubface was actually pointing to the right at impact.

Similarly, a shot which hooks left is caused by a clubface angle that is closed to the actual line of the swing at impact.

HEIGHT

The height on your golf shots is determined by the part of the ball that is struck, that is, the top, middle or bottom (see Figs 1.8 and 1.9). This is referred to as the angle of attack, the *plane* of the swing. If you hit the bottom of the ball, the club will inflict a lot of back-spin and the shot will have a high flight. Therefore, if your shots tend to go too high, your swing-plane is too steep and you are coming down on the ball. The top of the clubhead is contacting the bottom of the ball, thus creating excessive back-spin — creating a high, if not an actual 'sky' shot.

The important factor here isn't really what direction the ball starts off in, rather it is where the ball ends up! So spin is one of the big, big factors in golf. And to drive the point home, spin is caused by an open or closed clubface at impact.

LEARN TO 'LEFT-SPIN' THE BALL

The type of spin the great golfers inflict on the golf-ball is called a left-spin. It is the same as a conversion in rugby or soccer: when the player hits the ball, he drives it up into the air, swinging his leg from right to left, from inside to outside. And as the ball is in the air, it has slight left-spin, even though it is driven forwards and it is going to curve 'gently' towards the left at the end of the flight. This is the ideal flight for a

THE DRAW SHOT
Learn to play the right to left draw shot

maximum distance shot because the angle of attack will always be shallow — direct. If you are an habitual slicer the ball is going to be travelling (spinning) towards the right at the end. To inflict this type of spin you have to *swing* the club across the ball from the outside, and inevitably it will be a steeper swing and lack the penetration of the other swing. The force of the swing is going to go into the ground — downwards. If your shots are lacking distance and much too *high,* you are chopping the ball, your swing-plane is too *steep.*

AVOID THE BAD, BAD SHOTS!

There are what I call bad shots in golf, and there are bad, bad shots. There are two families of bad shots, one much worse than the other. If you are in the 'out to in' category of swinger, where you come at the ball from the outside, there are a possible six bad shots you can get (See chapter 2, page 51). The interesting thing here is that shots which seem to be quite different have a similar background. They could be called blood brothers. For example, you could set up on a tee, hit the ball from left to right and slice it. In other words, the ball ends up on the right-hand side of the fairway or in the rough. On the next tee you could make the same swing and the ball could go straight left (pull). The two shots seem totally different but they are in fact very similar. The slice is caused by an 'out to in' swing, swinging leftwards, and the clubface is open to the swing-line (slice right), but the second time the clubface is square to the swing-line (pull left) and the ball flies to the left. This can be very, very confusing. You may think there are two different swings involved here, but it really is just one factor that has changed — the angle of the clubface.

▶ BE AWARE OF LOFT ANGLE

An even more extraordinary thing is that you can have the same swing and the same angle and get different results by using different types of clubs. You can get a different shape on the club. For example, with the 3 Iron you can swing across the ball with an open clubface, getting a vicious slice, and then do exactly the same swing with your 8 Iron and the ball goes miles left (see Fig 5.2). Why is this? It is because the loft angle has a huge bearing on the spin of

Fig 5.2 If you were to use different lofted clubs and exactly the same swing for all, the flight patterns would inevitably be different, for example, the No 1 Driver could slice and the No 3 Wood could give a straighter shot.

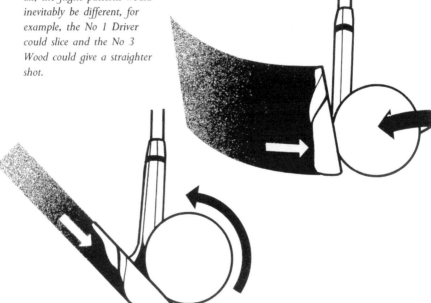

the golf-ball. With the 8 Iron, because of the angle on the face, it is the bottom of the face that strikes the bottom of the ball, and even if the face is slightly open it will always cause back-spin, so the ball will always go on a straight line. In contrast, with the 3 Iron and an open face, it's the middle of the face hitting the middle of the ball which will always give you right-spin. Where you have the same swing and the same clubface angle, by virtue of using different lofted clubs you will get huge variance in the flight patterns. You could hit your 3 Wood fairly straight because the angle on the Wood is more forgiving — the bottom of the face will contact the bottom half of the ball and create more back-spin. Try the same with the Driver and it will shoot viciously to the right. The 3 Wood is hiding a fault in your swing whereas the Driver is showing you that the clubface is slightly open to your swing-line. When someone says 'I'm hooking my Wedge and slicing my Driver', their swing has not changed at all.

Fig 5.3 Position of ball in (A) shows 'shank' impact; position of ball in (B) shows 'pull' impact.

a)

b)

So, if you wanted to find out whether you had an open or a closed clubface, or if your clubface was 'misbehaving', your low Irons would tell you. If you wanted to find out about your swing-line, your lofted 8s and 9s would tell you. The secret is to be able to accurately describe the shots you hit and then to define them. There are the bad, bad shots — the slice and the pull, the shank, sky, fluff and pull-hook. They represent one family of shots. For example, if you swing across from the outside and you slice the ball, you are also very likely to pull the ball to the left and get the odd sky shot. Now, if

83

you pull the ball with your arms to the left, it means you are coming across the ball from the outside and the ball is going to be hit quite near the shank of the club. Golfers who suffer from the 'shank shot' are original pullers of the ball, so the different varieties of shots are all coming from the same type of swing (see Fig 5.3). If you can get at the ball from the other angle, from the inside, and get your attack from inside to outside (as the soccer player does), there is a possibility that you can push the ball or hook it, or even push-slice it, but you cannot slice, pull or sky the ball from these positions (see Fig 5.4).

Fig 5.4 An 'out to in' swing (A) will give you six bad shots; an 'in to out' swing (B) will give a possible three bad shots.

a)

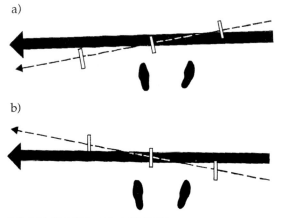

b)

▶ VARY YOUR PRACTICE

I was watching a champion golfer train during the winter. He came to the driving range night after night. I was amazed at his patience when practising. All around him golfers were 'slugging' the ball. In the three months I watched him practise, he never hit a full shot. He concentrated on punches, high fades, finesse shots all the time. This should be a lesson to you: you must get away from the power syndrome. Shape your play, get a handle on that ball. Nominate the shot you are going to play. Slow everything down — don't compete with the golfer in the next bay. Pattern your play. Learn ball control.

If you want to become a really class player, place yourself behind a tree or some obstacle, take out a 7/8 Iron and try manoeuvring the golf-ball around the tree.

What I mean is, try to hit the ball from right to left, then hit it from left to right, or alternatively chip it over the tree.

It is up to you to decide what shape of shot

you prefer. Try to get a pattern going and stick to it. The low handicap golfers like to 'draw' the ball with the long shots. You can certainly play golf with a controlled slice, but it's very unlikely that you will play off anything lower than a twelve handicap. If you can play the power fade or the power draw, you can play off anything you want really. If you want the maximum distance shot then you have got to learn to left-spin the ball.

HOW TO SELF-CORRECT AND BREAK AWAY FROM MEDIOCRITY

Here are some sample analyses you should make at the range or on the practice ground. You hit the ball and it goes along the ground — by analysing the flight you will find that the ball was struck on the very top (see Fig 1.9). Rather than ask 'What did I do wrong in my swing?', you've got to say 'I must hit the bottom of the ball, I must get

Fig 5.5 Your grip will determine the clubface angle at impact.

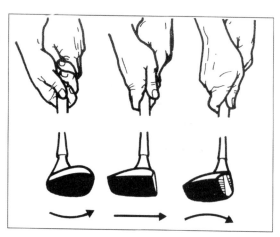

the clubhead to the other part of the ball'. If the ball goes way to the left, then you must

ask 'Why did the ball go left and hook more
left at the finish of the flight?' It was of
course because the clubface was closed to
your swing-line (see Fig 5.5). You must work
on the clubface angle. The clubface angle is
governed by your grip. Weaken your grip —
no knuckles should be visible on your left
hand — and fan the clubhead open as you
start back. Rotate your left arm in order to
do this on take-away. If you slice the ball,
you must deduce that you inflicted right-spin
on the ball, with an open clubface for a
steep outside angle. To cure this, you must
school yourself into presenting a closed
clubface at impact — alter your grip once
again and hood the clubface on take-away
(that is, keep it looking at the ball).

*Fig 5.6 Try to have the
clubface to the ball 'ahead'
of your hands.*

RELEASE THE CLUBHEAD

▶ DISTANCE

If your shots are lacking distance, then you are not compressing the ball at impact, you lack clubhead speed, you don't understand leverage — you must learn to waggle the clubhead at address and unlock that swing of yours. Go for an excessive wrist cock and a very early release. Try to have the clubface to the ball before your hands. The legendary American golfer Sam Snead once said: 'Feel that your wrists are oily — strike hard with your strong hand' (that is, your right hand). Work the stick — let the clubhead go at the ball. Follow the clubhead to achieve maximum distance with minimum effort. You must never become personally involved — let the clubhead take over.

'Power kick' the clubhead forward rather than the body. It is very difficult to power kick the clubhead forward and at the same time hold the top half of your body back. This is what is demanded in successful golf — to learn not to strike, but to allow the clubhead to do it for you.

Golf starts from a 'dead ball' situation. *You* are responsible for inflicting every aspect of flight on this 'dead ball'. To become a class player, you must develop a swing that works for you and analyse your game so as to be able to accurately describe and name your shot patterns, and immediately change the shape of your shots if there is a problem.

Fig 5.7 is a summary of the game of golf. It breaks the flight of the ball into separate compartments and analyses right back through the swing. If you are able to see the various compartments, you will have jumped right into the tournament player's mind. The following notes will help you interpret the chart.

SECTION A *(Read chart downwards)*

This section summarises how height is determined by swing plane.

If you set up with a strong left side and a compressed right side, you will automatically turn better, which ensures a wide backswing. Take advantage of this by swinging in with a shallow (rather than steep) attack and drive the ball away at the perfect elevation. The perfect angle of elevation for a drive is 45 degrees — this is directly due to the part of the ball you strike and to the plane of your attack. The plane of your attack is determined by your set-up.

SECTION B *(Read across from Section A)*

This section summarises how direction is determined by clubface angle.

If your shots are to fly straight, then the ball must have back-spin (not excessive) and your clubface must be square (not open or closed) at impact. This is directly due to your grip angle at impact. Your grip controls the clubface angle, it determines the degree of spin on the flight, and this creates the swerve on the shot.

SECTION C *(Read across from Section B)*

This section summarises how clubhead speed determines distance.

Fig 5.7 THE ULTIMATE SHO

Section A
SWING PLANE

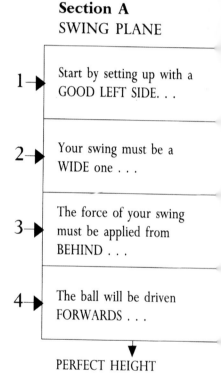

1 → Start by setting up with a GOOD LEFT SIDE. . .

2 → Your swing must be a WIDE one . . .

3 → The force of your swing must be applied from BEHIND . . .

4 → The ball will be driven FORWARDS . . .

PERFECT HEIGHT

The distance a ball travels is directly due to clubhead speed at impact. Clubhead speed comes from a swing that has leverage. A swing with leverage comes from 'oily wrists' at address — you sense 'fluidity' and loosen up your swing.

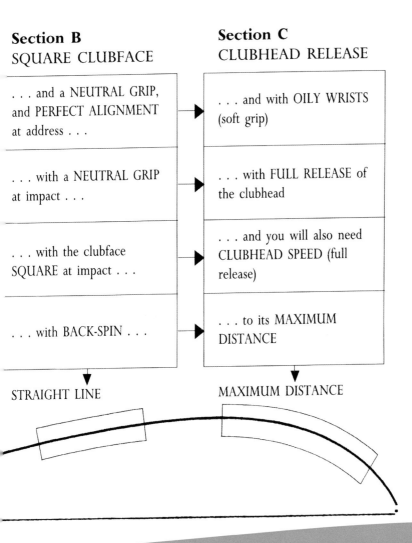

Section B SQUARE CLUBFACE	**Section C** CLUBHEAD RELEASE
. . . and a NEUTRAL GRIP, and PERFECT ALIGNMENT at address . . .	. . . and with OILY WRISTS (soft grip)
. . . with a NEUTRAL GRIP at impact . . .	. . . with FULL RELEASE of the clubhead
. . . with the clubface SQUARE at impact . . .	. . . and you will also need CLUBHEAD SPEED (full release)
. . . with BACK-SPIN . . .	. . . to its MAXIMUM DISTANCE

STRAIGHT LINE

MAXIMUM DISTANCE

'Golf is such a mad, stupid,
infuriating, crazy game,'
says the weekend player.
'You know I'm glad I don't
have to play again until
next Sunday!'

THE SHORT GAME

MASTERING THE SHORT GAME

In the long game you need 'accuracy' and
'distance'. You need a wide sweeping swing
with 'leverage'. In the short game you just
need accuracy. I call the short game the
'money department'. This is where you are
going to become a champion or fail. This is
it!

Fig 6.1 The short game

The clubs numbered 6, 7, 8, 9 and 10 and
the Sand Wedge are designed for shorter
play. It may be difficult to drive like Seve
Ballesteros or Nancy Lopez, but mastering
the short game is an attainable goal. You
should decide right now that you are going
to improve an area that requires no force —

simply accuracy. Become a demon chipper and putter and win, win, win! You need accuracy and height.

A startling statistic is that 65 per cent of all the shots you play are within a thirty-yard (27m) radius of the green. Now we are all capable of striking the ball thirty yards, even on our worst day. The question is, can we strike the ball accurately to a specific target? It is a very attainable short-range goal.

LEARN TO LOCK THE CLUBFACE TOWARDS THE FLAG AT IMPACT

These shots are mastered at the impact position where the clubface is square to the target precisely as it strikes the ball. What you must learn to do is to lock the clubhead to the target at impact, to magnetise one to the other. The clubface itself is like the barrel of a gun — you aim it, or like the front of your car — you face it in a certain direction and then you drive it.

Here is the sequence you must follow. Stand in a position where the ball is directly between you and the target and:

1. Aim the clubface at the target.

2. Aim your feet, hips and shoulders slightly left of the target — open to the target line.

3. Place the ball well back in your stance — this ensures a downward blow on the ball with the Iron and a square position with your shoulders. Now 'pinch' the ball — take a divot. A lot of people make the mistake of trying to scoop the ball. You have to hit down on the ball in the short game and let the loft of the club bring

the ball up. You need height and you will only achieve this by striking down on the ball (it's a game of opposites!). Once you do this, the ball will begin to pop up for you and sit down on the green, beside the flag.

Fig 6.2 (left) The clubhead is being lined up with the target at address.

Fig 6.3 (right) The follow-through, keeping the clubface square to the target.

4. Keep most of your weight on the forward foot. It must remain there for the duration of the swing. This prevents swaying — moving off the ball.

5. Above all, play with 'dead hands'. Take the small muscles — the hands and wrists — out of the swing. Keep your swing stiff and in one piece. Use a very short backswing and extend triangle to target. The short backswing ensures an acceleration through the swing, even over the short distance.

Fig 6.4 For Wedge shots you need a steep swing. Use a second ball during practice to ensure a steep, sharp attack on the ball.

"Chop the chip"

Use the 'L' swing (modified of course). Strike it down on the ball using some of the 'V' swing, and keeping the back of your left hand and the clubhead locked onto the target.

When a golfer complains about the short game, I immediately suspect his/her grip. You need a 'gentle touch' close to the green. Compare it to playing a piano — you play with your fingertips, never with the palms of your hands. Your right-hand grip is all about 'delicacy' and 'feel'. You don't strike the ball — you 'finesse' it. If you 'fist' (palm) the right-hand grip — forget it. Look at Fig 3.6. The right hand is out of its normal position; it will automatically revert back to its normal position and close the clubface at impact, thus preventing the essential height on the shot. A hooker's grip is simply disastrous for the short game. Players who are inflicted with this type of grip have to resort to a kind of scooping action around the green.

▶ PRACTICE ROUTINES

1. Straightforward pitch shot. Back of left hand to the flag

A good way to practise this shot is to get an umbrella, open it out and put it into the ground, twenty yards or so (18m) away from you. Pitch the ball into the brolly and work your way out gradually to longer shots. The secret here is to work out your alignment. You can do this by placing two clubs on the ground, one pointing directly towards the target, the other club slightly open to that line (left). Place the clubhead between the two clubs and then swing, making sure you hit down on the ball, getting the necessary height on it and getting the feeling of locking the clubhead to the target precisely at impact. As you move out from the umbrella, you progress up the shaft of the club and you lengthen your backswing slightly. A general rule of thumb — try to make the length of your forward swing twice that of your backswing. Get the feeling of a controlled backswing, and that you are hitting down and through the ball. If you use a very long backswing when you only need to drive the ball a very short distance, you will inevitably have a decelerating hit through the ball, usually resulting in a 'fluff' shot. I always remember working at a club which had a Par 5 in front of the shop. Golfers would hit two good wooden shots up near the green. They would take a driver-like backswing (complete overswing) for this thirty-yard (27m) shot and stick the club in the ground. My advice to someone with such a huge overswing would be: it's a swing I want, not an event. You have got to get a shorter backswing. You must realise that a shorter backswing allows for an accelerating forward swing even over a very short distance. You must attack the chip. Hit it down and through. In other words, don't be afraid to accelerate the clubhead through the ball. Short, back, down and through. If you cannot play this shot, you cannot play golf!

Fig 6.5 For the straightforward pitch shot, play the ball back in your stance and swing the back of your left hand towards the flag.

2. 'Cut up' shot. Extreme height on flight of ball over a short distance

This is what I call 'a must shot' — a shot where there is no other alternative. You are confronted with a bunker in your direct line to the pin, or some other similar type of hazard. The type of shot you must pull off is a very high one over a short distance and one that will 'sit down' quickly on the green. You must develop a technique of holding the clubface open as you slide it underneath the ball and finish with the clubface facing skywards (open) at the end of the swing. Don't close it!

Here is how it works (see Figs 6.6, 6.7, 6.8):

Fig 6.6 (left) Cut-up shot: use 'open' stance and aim clubface at target.

Fig 6.7 (centre) Swing 'out to in' along the feet line.

Fig 6.8 (right) Swing from outside 'across' the ball through impact, holding the clubface open.

● Aim your feet, hips and shoulders left of target (open stance). Aim the clubface at the target (clubface will be laid open). Play the ball opposite your left foot (forward in your stance).

● Using your right hand swing the club up very steeply. A definite 'V' type swing, and slightly outside going back, fanning the clubface open at the same time.

We call it the 'GLASS ACT'
Imagine a glass sitting on the clubface through impact

● The swing is from outside, across the ball through impact, with the clubface open or pointing skywards. Slide the clubhead underneath the ball.

It is a brilliant shot, but a very difficult one. It is interesting to note that even though the Sand Wedge face is very open at impact — it is the bottom edge (which is forward) that will strike the bottom of the ball — the ball will not fly right as with the Driver or Iron, but straight up, in a straight line.

You must aim your feet very much left of target, but aim the clubface directly at the target. Open it out. It is an 'all or nothing' shot. If you are going to play the shot, you must not 'chicken out' of it. Make sure you hit down and through the ball, following through to the end. Confidence is the key factor here. Convince yourself that you can play the shot, that you are good around the greens, that this is one of your better shots. Just before you commence your swing, lighten your grip, soften it, and swing longer and slower than you normally do. Make sure you do not stop at the ball. Swing right through it. Full follow-through.

THE BUNKER

The bunker is probably the area most feared by beginner golfers and a lot of handicap golfers. Your swing here must be 'out to in' with an open face. You 'slice' the ball out of the sand. The Sand Wedge is a club apart from the rest. It was designed specifically for the sand shot. Gene Sarazen, a legendary American golfer, told of how in 1933, while taking flying lessons, he pulled the control stick back, and as a consequence the tail-flaps went down and the nose simultaneously moved upwards. He related these actions to the principle of sand play. If the trailing edge of the Sand Wedge were lower than the leading edge, the club would cut through the sand more effectively, allowing for an explosion shot without the digging action of the conventional niblick. This is how the Sand Wedge was born. Forty-one years later, at the 126-yard (115m) eighth hole, known as the postage stamp, on Troon Golf Course, while playing in the 1973 British Open Championship, Gene Sarazen holed out his tee shot. Remarkable!

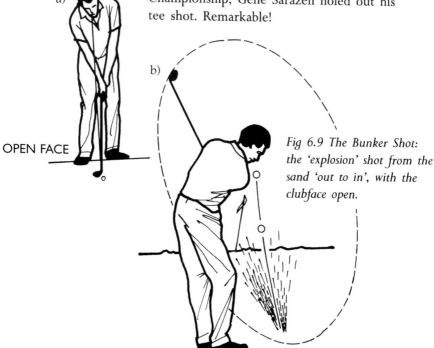

a)

OPEN FACE

b)

Fig 6.9 The Bunker Shot: the 'explosion' shot from the sand 'out to in', with the clubface open.

► THE BUNKER SHOT

It is important to realise that sand, being loose in texture, will react differently from soil. (See Fig 6.10) The main problem with bunker shots is when the clubface closes, so allowing the sand to accumulate in front of it, causing a 'fluffed shot'. Remember, the Sand Wedge was never meant to be used as a bulldozer.

The same technique applies to the sand shot as to the cut-up shot we have just described. You aim your feet, hips and shoulders left of the target. (See Fig 6.6.) You aim the clubhead at the target. In order to do this, the clubhead must be laid wide open. (See Fig 6.9(a).) You should aim the clubhead about two inches (5cm) behind the ball. The swing must be 'out to in' or across the ball, keeping the face open or pointing skywards all the time. Try to get the feeling of keeping your body very, very steady as you strike and of sliding the clubhead underneath the ball rather than against it. Imagine there is an insect under the ball holding it up and you are going to cut the legs from under him (see Fig 6.9(b)). Handicap players are often tempted to look at the outcome of the shot before it is actually completed.

Where bunker shots are concerned, the need to keep the head still throughout the exercise cannot be overstated. Remember, once you hit the golf-ball it is history. You just have to wait for the result. The exercise of exploding a ball out of sand demands considerably more power than the inexperienced player might imagine. Beginners have a tendency to consider only the relatively short distance the ball may be required to travel from a green-side trap. Because of the high resistance, however, a full shot is absolutely vital. Use the explosion technique. The explosion shot should be played with the same tempo as that required to extract a ball from heavy rough.

The steep bunker shot

The situation will arise where you have a very steep bunker and a very short distance

Fig 6.10 Use your feet as 'educators' in the sand. If the sand is hard the ball flies out; if the sand is loose the ball will come out slowly.

to go. In this situation you should open the clubface even more, take the club up much quicker (steeper) and, keeping the clubface open, slide it underneath the ball — what I would call a severe version of the 'V' swing. You just pop it out!

The long bunker shot

The long bunker shot is the most difficult shot in golf. This is a speciality shot. The secret here is to school yourself into 'plucking' the ball from the sand. In other words, don't muck around with the sand. Get this ball out as clean as a whistle. Visualise the impact position. You have to feel that you are 'half' blading the ball — aim at the middle of the ball and get the feeling that, at impact, you are keeping your hands back and you are letting the clubhead go past your hands. It is very important to take a sufficiently lofted club, one that will ensure that the ball will clear the edge of the bunker. This shot requires plenty of practice.

Ball buried in sand

Occasionally you will be confronted with a ball that is buried in the sand. In this instance you have to reverse the technique adopted for the other shots: you must close the clubface and just swing the club back, bringing it down on top of the ball, keeping the face closed, with no follow-through whatsoever, and the ball will come out. When it hits the green, it will have quite an amount of top-spin on it. This shot is used to get the ball out of the bunker — it does not allow you to aim directly at the hole.

Fig 6.11 (above) Ball buried in the sand — a poached egg.

Fig 6.12 Close the clubface at impact.

The 7 Iron pitch-and-run — the money shot

We have practised a few specialist shots which require a high level of skill. Now we will try a very practical shot and a simple one, one that you should use as often as you possibly can — the 7 Iron pitch-and-run shot.

Think of this shot as a long putt. Aim the clubface once again at the target. Play the ball well back in the stance and just swing the club up and down the line, keeping the back of your left hand going to the target. Try this practice routine: hold the club so that the shaft is in the position shown in Fig 6.13. If you swing and flick your wrists, or turn it over, the shaft will strike off your side. To prevent this happening you must school yourself into leading with your hands. Lock the clubhead once again to the target. Play this shot as often as you can as it is a relatively safe shot. Remember, there is a 'jingle' in this shot.

Fig 6.13 (opposite) The shaft on the ground indicates ball position for the 7 Iron pitch-and-run shot.

▶ ESSENTIALS

1. Keep telling yourself you have a great short game — even convince your friends! Act as if you already are a great short-game player.

2. Check the position of your right-hand grip. Ensure that you are not fisting it. 'Finesse' the ball with your fingers.

3. Alignment — clubface to flag.

4. Practise, practise, practise your short game (even in your garden!).

" Position ball hook in your stance for the short chip and run shots."

Remember, 65 per cent of golf is your short game. If you were running your own business and one client was responsible for 65 per cent of all your custom, how well would you look after that client?

MEMBERSHIP DRIVE
Cypress Point, USA, an ultra-private club, is reported to have only 240 members. It sees almost no play. Bob Hope, a member for forty years, is reported to have said, 'One year we had a big membership drive — and drove out fifty members!'

PUTTING

A GAME WITHIN A GAME

Putting is one part of golf where the golf-ball never leaves the ground. Forty-three per cent of the shots you take during a round of golf will be on the green. The putt is the shot that demands precise accuracy. You don't need strength to strike the ball on the green, so there is no excuse for you not being a good putter. It is the one area of the game which should allow you to say to Jack Nicklaus or Nick Faldo or any of the greats: 'Let's see if I can take you on the putting green.'

Golf was not always played towards a 'hole'. Early Dutch players aimed the ball towards a stick in the ground. The stick was continually being removed by 'unseen' hands and, having eventually tired of replacing it, the players simply played the ball into the hole that remained. There are many players today who would wish the sticks used at that time had been bigger! The actual size of the golf hole is four and a half inches (11.5cms) wide. It is the same size as a cigarette packet. If someone were to ask you to strike a ball and hit a cigarette packet from a radius of two to three feet (0.5m to 1m), you would have absolutely no problem. However, when we think of it as a hole in the ground, it becomes a major problem.

The American golfer **Lee Trevino** once said: 'You have to feel that you are a great putter in order to be one'

A 'MUST' PUTT — HOW TO PERFORM IN COMPETITION

" I am a great putter!"

Have you ever had to play a very important putt? A ten-foot (3m) putt in a big match at a crucial time in the round? Does the following description bring back memories?

You are standing over the ball, you are concentrating very hard, you *must* hole it. You are somehow aware of your partner's glare, the opposition have that 'hope you lip it out far away' look on their faces. You study the line again. Your body is tight. You settle on a line — you think! You strike the putt, 'wishing' it in. You are two separate people — one hoping, the other hitting.

The ball lips out. You have missed! Suddenly your whole body deflates in disappointment. You move up towards the hole and tap the ball in. Your playing partners have already charged on to the next tee. You look at the putt again and wonder what happened. What went wrong? You think, 'If only I could hit it again!' You can't resist! You place the ball in approximately the same spot. This time you are under no pressure. It doesn't really matter. You couldn't care less, and what's more, no one else could either! You knock the putt straight into the hole. You wonder, 'now, why couldn't I have done that the first time?'

Why is it you always succeed second time around? The answer — the pressure! What do I mean by the pressure? You are 'one person' second time around. You are not 'hoping' and 'hitting' the putt. You are merely hitting it. It's just like breathing, walking, talking — you never consider how you breathe, how you talk, you just get on with it. The conscious mind is missing the second time around. You are no longer afraid, no longer pleading with yourself, 'I must hole it! I must hole it! I must hole it!'. Unknowingly, when you struck the second putt with a 'devil may care' attitude, you used only the miraculous 'subconscious' mind and body as *one*. There was no division the second time. You acted before you thought. You could see the whole picture clearly. In the 'must' putt, the essence of the person (you) was trapped, unable to express itself. Your 'head' got in the way. There is a very old saying: 'If you think for too long, you'll hit it wrong!'

THE 'POSITIVE' APPROACH

You are hoping to become a great putter one day. Here is a blueprint for a new approach to putting:

1. Write down exactly how good a putter you would like to become.

2. Then get a tape recorder and record yourself making these three points:
   'From now on my worries are over.'
   'I am a successful putter.'
   'I now control my own thoughts, and only think about the positive things I 'want' to happen.

3. Now the crucial point. Act as if you already are a great putter. Say to yourself: 'I have a beautiful putter, a lovely smooth stroke. I am a wonderful putter. The ball

'I am a great putter'

Fig 7.1 If you think positively you will be surprised at the results.

PUTTING

The secret of success in many spheres of life is to follow instinct rather than reason. To Act before you Think. This is typical of high handicappers on the green.

A friend of mine watched this man standing over a putt for six minutes. 'What in the name of heaven is he doing?' asked his playing partner. His opponent said, 'He must be praying!' His partner replied, 'I think he finished praying a while ago, he must now be waiting for a bloody answer!'

rolls beautifully for me....' This is so important. It is based on the simple premise that believing you have it is the first stage, the natural step — the physical reality follows on from this.

4. Always keep updating your script. Make a tape of it. Play it over and over to yourself, especially just before you play a round of golf. Let it all become programmed into your subconscious mind — don't *try* to listen, just listen in a relaxed way.

5. See yourself all the time as feeding your mind with positive thoughts, weeding out the negative ones. The word 'worry' comes from an Anglo-Saxon word meaning to 'choke'. So, you must not allow negative thoughts to choke your putts. Always speak positively about your putting. Programme yourself so that you will always 'think' positively.

" I am a great putter!"

Switch from − to +

Avoid negative thinking, golfers who condemn themselves to bad putting. As you become more positive, the hole acts like a magnet to attract good luck — putts start to drop in from all angles. Continually feed your mind with positive thoughts. Don't allow any old thought to enter and dwell in your mind — only allow positive ones to enter. If you are able to grasp this simple

Fig 7.2 The hole should act as a magnet to the ball.

approach, you have made one of the greatest discoveries of your life — that golfers can alter their scores on the green dramatically, simply by switching their thought patterns from negative to positive. Your putting score is formed by the thoughts that habitually occupy your mind.

" I am a great putter!"

► A FEW SIMPLE RULES

- Do not take too long looking over your putts. If you do, you will only arouse programmed fears and anxieties, which in turn will produce rigor mortis and panic.

- Never think about *how* you are going to strike any putt.

- Give your total concentration to *where* you want the ball to go.

- Understand that improvement on the green comes about, not by making a supreme effort, but by ceasing all effort. Change from 'hitting and hoping' to merely 'hitting'. Once you do this, your awareness will increase dramatically.

- Look only once at the line to the hole. That 'picture' will stay with you.

- Now trust your instinct and strike the putt. Trust yourself to 'hole' it.

The things we do best are the things we are not aware of doing. Just 'Hole the putt! Hole the putt! Hole the putt!'.

ON THE PRACTICE GREEN

Some people call putting 'a game within a game'. As you practise and become a good technician on the green, you have to ask yourself: What is the key to it? What is it that I am looking for? In the long game you are looking for accuracy and distance. On the green, you are concerned only with accuracy. Do you need leverage? No! No wrist action, no moving parts!

You must develop a sound technique. The triangle moves together. The elbows move together. The shoulders move together. The weight is forward on the left foot and stays there for the duration of the stroke. Eyes are over the ball. Stroke is 'in to out'. Backswing should be half the distance (short) of the forward stroke. This stroke is sometimes

'WHO CARES?'
The actor Jack Lemmon, playing in the Crosby USA, slashed the ball nine times before he reached the eighteenth green at Pebble Beach. As he lined up his putt for a ten, he asked his caddie, 'Which way does it break?' 'Who cares!' replied the caddie.

113

referred to as the pendulum method. Pick a spot in front of the line and hit the ball.

" I am a great putter!"

Wait for the sound of the ball dropping into the hole. Don't look up — once you've hit the ball, it's history (let's hope it goes down in the annals as one of the great putts of our time!). Try to make a loud noise with your putter at impact. Lift the putter head up after impact, holding it over the line to the hole. I believe that the forward strike must be made with the right hand. Right hand pushes right through — a short backswing with a long, long follow-through. An upswing stroke. Get the ball rolling early. A steep and choppy swing will make the ball bounce on the green and it will always come up short.

Fig 7.3 Use the 'pendulum' method while putting.

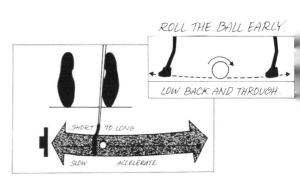

114

TACKLING THE COURSE

The legendary English golfer Henry Cotton once remarked: 'OK, he can strike the ball, but can he play the game?' In the final analysis, it is always the score that counts.

'I SHUDDA HAD A 63'
Two pals meet up. John has not seen Pat for a while. Pat was a keen fisherman. John enquires, 'How are you keeping and how's the fishing?' Pat replies, 'Oh, I gave up the fishing. I play the golf now and I enjoy it, like you said I would.'
'Great,' says John, 'but why did you give up the fishing?' Pat answers, 'Well, I finally realised that golf liars don't have to show anything!'

The golfer is born again every time he/she stands on the first tee. Playing a round of golf is like going on a journey. The player approaches every game with renewed optimism, in anticipation of that magic touch. Is there a secret to it all? The following will certainly help:

PREPARE WELL

Before heading off into the competition or into a game, set yourself up well. When you are having pre-game thoughts, visualise yourself playing well. Look forward to the game. Winners and losers think differently.

A loser sees the problem, a winner sees an opportunity. Be cautious with your club selection on the golf course. Avoid the 3 Iron, the Wood, etc, in tight lies. Once you are cautious with your selection you can afford to be optimistic about your shots.

The secret (if there is one) is to use your handicap and play within your present ability. Improve your ability only on the driving range. If you cannot pull a shot off on the practice range, don't try it on the course.

Winners and losers think differently.

It's extremely important to know when *not* to try a shot, to get into the mind of the course architect, to study the make-up of a golf course. Look at the score card — the normal card has ten par 4s, four par 3s and four par 5s. Therefore you need fourteen good tee shots, an average of fifty-six shots within a thirty yard (27m) radius of the green, and the rest long Irons and fairway Woods.

Study the indices on the score card and mark the holes where you have your shots.

If you are playing a strange course it is very important that you study the back of the card and look for local rules, like out-of-bounds areas and so forth, which may be pertinent to that particular course — the danger holes. Sometimes it is a good idea to get out and walk a few holes before the game.

Always arrive early, well before tee-off time, and hit a few shots. A friend of mine complained that he was 7 over par for the first nine holes and 1 under for the back nine. I explained to him that he had only warmed up on the back nine. If he had done his pre-game warm-up routine he would have played well throughout. The early swings in a round of golf need a lot of oil to make the swing fluid. You must think of this — your muscles will be cold and tight unless you do a warm-up.

It is also important to dress well — this will help you to feel better and, consequently, you will play better golf.

On the practice area, start with your Wedge to give your muscles a chance to warm up. Always finish with a few wooden shots because the first shot you will play will be a tee shot and a few good tee shots will set up a good round.

Avoid the pitfalls on the course. Remember that each shot is the only shot you have, so you must make the right decision.

Do firmly believe you have a 'deadly' short game.

REMEMBER THE FOLLOWING
POINTS:

Take advantage of the tee

When we stand on a tee we are being given
an advantage — we are allowed to tee the
ball up. My advice is: tee the ball up, well
up in the air. When I see a player tee really
low, I know instantly that he has problems.
He is afraid of the high tee because his
swing is too steep. If you are given an
advantage in life you should always take it.
Tee the ball up really high, learn to widen
your swing and sweep the ball away — take
it clean. Leave the tee in the ground and
keep practising this. A narrow, steep swing
will be quickly shown up.

Maintain a 'soft' grip on the club

When we stand on the tee, we are inclined
to focus on the flag on the green. We are
hypnotised by it. It seems a long distance
away so we gather ourselves for a mighty
effort to drive the ball an enormous
distance. Force becomes an instant issue.
This leads to a tighter grip and muscle
tension in the body. The secret here is not
to squeeze the blood out of your hands by
holding too tightly. Someone once asked
Arnold Palmer: 'What is inside a golf ball?'
He replied: 'The centre is wrapped in rubber
that is almost as tense as most golfers who
try to hit it!' Muscles need blood. Bloodless
hands are lifeless hands. Softly, softly with
the hands, is the secret of the masters. As
they say: 'Don't force the feel — feel the
force.' To soften the hands, to rid them of
tension, try banging them together hard, five

or six times, then go back to the club. You will notice your hands are relaxed again. To develop a smooth, even tempo, you need a 'soft' grip.

Favour the loft over distance

When you knock down your tee shot you feel embarrassed and annoyed. You instinctively feel that a superhuman effort is required in order to amend the wrong, to try to save the day, and so the power syndrome takes over. My advice in this instance is: react in the opposite way to how you instinctively feel, and if there is a conflict between loft and distance, always favour loft. Under pressure, in any situation, when things are not going the way they should be — the machine is not working correctly — we try to slow it down and see what the problem is. It is the very same in golf. If you knock down a tee shot into semi-rough, you should probably take out a 7 or 8 Iron and play the ball down the fairway. A keen golfer friend of mine revealed the secret behind his Captain's Prize win by telling me that he never played for the green. If he missed the small green the hazards were very severe. So he played his second shot up in front of the green and this left him with a very straightforward third shot. He out-foxed the golf course. Golf is a thinking person's game. As the saying goes: 'The six inches between the ears are the most important.'

'Sweep' the wood away

The wooden shot is your first shot. The wood is a flat-faced club. You have got to avoid a 'V' type swing (see chapter 1). A lot

Fig 8.1 A closed stance will give you maximum distance at address. Put your right foot slightly behind your left foot.

of the great players adopt a slightly closed stance on the drive. (See Fig 8.1.) This means that their right foot is back and the left foot is forward. They are thinking about

LEARN the 'draw' shot

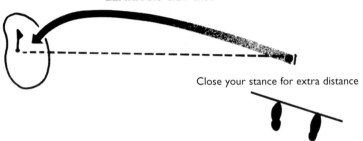

Close your stance for extra distance

a 'wide' type of swing, looking at the back of the ball and creating width, and holding it. In other words, sweeping the ball clean and leaving the tee in the ground. You must learn to strike the wood on your upswing.

Fig 8.2 Hit the ball with the Driver on the upswing for maximum distance.

Hit it up to heaven

'Delicate' power gives results

Your tempo is very, very important in golf. If you are driving a nail into wood, an accurate strike with the hammer is much more effective than a massive stroke. (See Fig 2.10.) So it is with golf. A good, even tempo, working the machine and hitting the ball accurately, will drive the ball enormous distances.

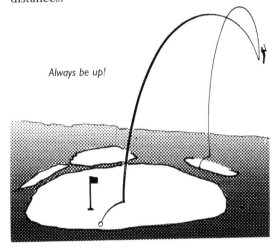

Always be up!

Fig 8.3 A lot of golfers think they are stronger than they actually are! They are disappointed when the ball lands short in the bunker. If this happens to you, try using one extra club, for example, an 8 rather than a 9 Iron.

Know your clubs

This is also very important. For example, avoid playing a 3 Iron off a tight lie. A 5 Wood or a 7 Wood is much easier. As a general rule you should put your pride in your pocket if you want to win. Play with the club you are happiest with, and play the shot you feel will lead you closer to the pin — whatever that may be. A 130-yard (119m) shot could be a punch with a 6 Iron — it doesn't always have to be a full 9 Iron.

Avoid the 'common' errors

In their approach shots to the green, golfers make two fundamental errors:

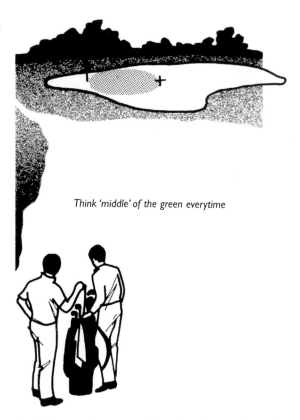

Fig 8.4 Do not become hypnotised by the flag. Play for the centre of the green and you will have better results.

Think 'middle' of the green everytime

1. They are hypnotised by the flag and tend to go directly for it instead of looking on the green as a whole, complete unit. You should play for the centre of the green most of the time. (See Fig 8.4.)

2. The second common fault is under-clubbing — coming up short. Always play an attacking shot past the pin. Another fault allied to this is over-swinging and a tendency to 'fluff' the ball. I always tell golfers: you will never get a medal for striking a 9 Iron 150 yards (137m) but you might get a prize if you can land the ball on the centre of the green near the flag. There are no medals for distance in golf!

GOLF IS A THREE MINUTE GAME!

A lot of golfers put themselves under undue pressure, especially beginners. They try to concentrate all the time during the round — they tend to mix up concentration with tension. You may spend four hours playing a round of golf and at least another hour talking about it in the bar, but it takes only two seconds to play each stroke. So you are playing golf for approximately three minutes! It is during these three minutes that you should focus on the round of golf.

SEE THE GOLDEN LINE

Fig 8.5 Try not to think of what might go wrong with your shot. Instead, use 'narrow vision' and focus on the middle of the green.

Concentration is seeing the shot and playing it without interference from the conscious mind, like breathing, talking, etc. Act before you think!

You only need to concentrate as you are playing the shot — in between times you should relax. I call this 'narrow vision' and 'wide vision'. As you walk down the fairway

Aim the clubface down at the target

Fig 8.6 To get correct alignment, you must aim the clubhead directly at the target and align your body parallel to the left of the target.

you should have wide vision, take it all in. You might check out parallel holes, smell the flowers. As the charismatic American golfer Walter Hagen once said on the way round: 'As you arrive at your ball, change to narrow vision, go behind the ball, see the shot.'

Know your distance — you should know to within a few feet exactly how far you should strike each shot with each club. Develop a personal Distance Chart. There is only the ball and the green. You aim the scoring part of the club, the clubhead, at the target and you sweep the ball to it. See the tunnel. Once you have played the shot, relax again and revert back to wide vision.

ACT AS IF YOU ALREADY ARE A GOOD GOLFER!

To really enjoy golf, you must have inner confidence. Quietly remind yourself that you are a good player, that you enjoy the game, that you like practising, that you have a great short game. Always wish the very best to your opponents. Be big. Play the course rather than your opponent. Encourage your playing partner and wish him/her well. Compliment them on a good shot. If you are a beginner you should study etiquette. A lot of it is common sense — respect for your golfing friends and for the golf course. Become a brisk player. Don't be too hard on yourself! — as a beginner, when you are not playing in competitions, tee the ball up if you are out on the fairway.

▶ DEVELOP A ROUTINE

One cannot stress enough the importance of developing a routine on the golf course, and you can do this by practising setting up to the ball in exactly the same way every time. Try to repeat everything you do, even the way you walk. Take your time, walk slowly and do exactly the same in each golf game — get into a routine. Your swing will become routine and your play will become more consistent.

▶ HOW TO SCORE WELL IN WINDY CONDITIONS

You can judge the wind in several ways: observe the trees, flag or pin, or toss a pinch of grass into the air. Alternatively, learn from other players' shots.

Into the wind: Take a less lofted club than usual. Aim the clubhead at the target and into the wind. Always position your body ahead of the ball — opposite your right foot.

Fig 8.7 a) When playing against the wind use a less lofted club and play the ball back in your stance; b) When playing with the wind use a more lofted club and position the ball forward in your stance.

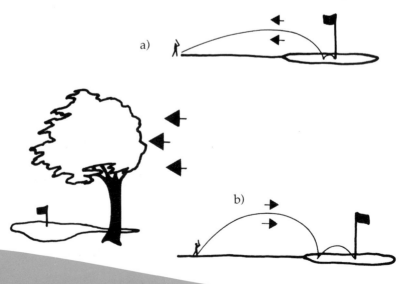

Move the weight onto your left foot and play the shot by swinging the hook of your left hand to the target. Play past the pin.

With the wind: Use a more lofted club than normal. Tee the ball higher. If driving, you could use a 3 Wood to get the ball airborne. It will go just as far as the Driver. Aim the clubhead at your target, play the ball forward in your stance, keep the weight back on your right foot, hit the ball 'up to heaven', and hit the ball with the clubhead on the upswing.

In a crosswind: Take a less lofted club than usual. Allow for the wind to affect the ball's flight and aim the clubhead at the intended target. If the wind is against you, try to keep the ball down. If the wind is helping you, try to get the ball up into the wind and use it to your advantage.

In windy conditions you should generally use your hands more, go for a 'wristier' swing, and if there are gale force winds on the green you must tap the putt using a stroke. Adopt the Byron Nelson motto: *'Make the wind your friend.'* Generally adopt a wider than normal stance in order to anchor yourself. Try to swing less and hit more.

HOW TO PLAY FROM UNEVEN LIES

You will come up against uneven lies on the golf course. Generally speaking, if the hill is going away from you and you are standing above the ball, the flight will also go away from you — the ball will go left to right. (See Fig 8.8(a).) If the hill is coming back towards you, the ball will tend to go right to left. (See Fig 8.8(b).) In these instances you must make sure you take plenty of loft in the club and make allowances. If the ball is

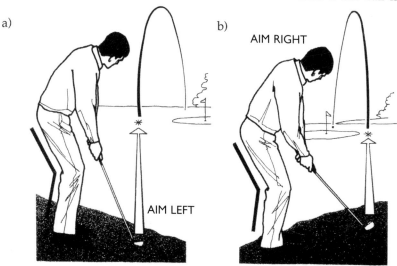

a)

b)

AIM RIGHT

AIM LEFT

Fig 8.8
a) Side-hill lie
When you play from the side of a hill and the ball is below your feet, make sure you aim to the left of the target, as the ball will travel from left to right.

b) When the ball is above your feet aim to the right of the target, as the ball will travel from right to left.

below your feet you have to aim left; if the ball is above your feet, aim right. When confronted with a shot from an uneven lie, avoid a full swing, that is, a driving range one. Waggle the clubhead, allow for the slope and flick the ball away. Play a 'hands only' shot.

Above all, approach your golf with the correct mentality. I will leave you with a number of what I consider to be key points in this regard:

1. You must have a repetitive thought pattern. In other words, you can't be in a dither going out to play golf — forget it.

2. Picture the shot mentally before swinging a club. The better the picture of the shot in the mind, the greater the chance of

accomplishing it. Your attitude must be one of expectation, not of doubt. When putting, for example, picture yourself actually picking the ball out of the hole.

3. Make a list of a few key swing thoughts. Choose one key thought each day and concentrate positively on it. It is impossible to contend with more than one key idea at any one time.

4. Watch your alignment (see Fig 8.6.) It is just as important to think about tactics as about swing. How often have you seen a golfer making a perfect swing but never taking account of the alignment? He aims in the wrong direction or takes the wrong club. He hits a great shot but ends up either thirty yards (27m) short of or forty yards (36m) past the green.

5. In developing your own particular style, try to model yourself on some player who has the same stature as yourself.

6. Always relax between each shot. It can help to ameliorate or alter particular problems which arise between shots. It is to your advantage if you can direct your mind away from the pressure of the moment. Tension can pose difficulties for the golfer. I'd like to share with you a little ploy which you may find helpful. Before you strike the ball, tighten every muscle as hard as you can, gripping the club with all your might. Then relax. If you use this formula it will help dispel pent-up tension in the system. You will then be 'ready to play'.

'WHAT DOG?'

This story exemplifies the terror that consumes most amateurs when playing tournament golf.

The actor Jack Lemmon was about to drive when out of the gallery tore a big scruffy dog. It ran straight through Lemmon's legs and disappeared into the crowd on the other side of the tee. Without batting an eye, Lemmon played a fine tee shot.

Jim Demaret, doing commentary after the round, went up to Jack and said, 'Jack, that was really remarkable composure you displayed back there on the fifteenth tee. That dog ran right between your legs and you didn't let it disturb you at all!'

Lemmon looked at Demaret in complete surprise, and said, 'You mean that was a real dog?'

7. Will power and determination are fundamental ingredients in effecting positive progress in your performance. Perhaps it is this quality of will power which marks the demarcation line between the great and the ordinary. As the American psychologist Emerson once said: *'They conquer who believe they can.'*

History of the Game

8

The name golf is sometimes thought to derive from the German word Kolbe (club) and may be a Celtic version of it.

The first known instance of a game resembling golf was a game called pagawica, which was played by Roman soldiers using a curved club and a leather ball stuffed with feathers. The Romans who came to conquer Britain occupied parts of Scotland and England from about 55 B.C. to A.D. 409. However, it must be emphasised that there is no direct evidence to suggest that pagawica was in any way related to golf. A similar game to golf, called cambuca, was played in England with a wooden ball but there is no certainty as to the kind of club that was used to hit the ball. It probably was similar to the kind of club used in pagawica. There was an illustration of a game of golf showing a figure striking the ball, on a stained glass window in Gloucester Cathedral, as far back as the year 1310. According to historical

"BLESS MY SOUL, ZORG, HE THINKS YOU'RE SOME KIND OF GOD"

antiquity on this particular depiction, it is accepted that the figure shown is a golfer in action. In France around the same period, there is evidence of a similar game which was called chole, being played. It, too, consisted of hitting the ball with a club towards some fixed point.

Many people believe that golf originated in Scotland and, of course, there are many claims by Scottish writers to this effect. That well-known Scottish literary figure, Robert Browning, in his **History of Scotland,** makes a strong case in defence of his claim. However, it is now widely recognised that it was Dutch who invented the modern game and called it the first time Kolf. The origin of golf as we know it today can be traced back to a little village in Holland, called **Leonan.** There is evidence which suggests that the game was played there as far back as 1296. Those same records show proof of the establishment of as many as thirty or more centres where Kolf was played. In wintertime, the game was played on ice. In numerous Dutch paintings from the period as shown, people are depicted playing golf in open spaces. Apparently, the game was quite popular between the period 1300-1700, but in the early part of the 18th century, the game died out. It wasn't until 1890 the game was revived after centuries of neglect in Holland. This revival was due interestingly to a group of Scottish golfers who opened a club and course at the Hague. Golf had returned once more to its true roots.

With regard to the history of the game in Scotland, it is of significance that golf was to appear on the east coast, and can be directly attributable to the close trading links between both countries. When the seas receded around the coastline on the east of Scotland, there were wild undulating pastures unsuitable for agricultural purposes, but ideal for golf course lay-out. In these early stages, the golfer had to share the 'commons' with fishermen drying nets, women drying clothes, footballers at play, the army on manoeuvres and many other competing interests. *(See diagram 159).*

The rich and poor mingled on what came to be known as the seaside 'commons'. This particular mingling of the classes was to be particularly significant in that the aristocratic golfer was prepared to fight and pay for the legal battles which were fought in order to preserve the land for everyone's use.

The slow progress in the development of the game in Scotland could be related to the type of ball being used. It was a leather ball stuffed with feathers "the feathery". This was the kind of ball along with specially made wooden clubs which were used by the King and his nobles. This majority of people used a more simple kind of wooden

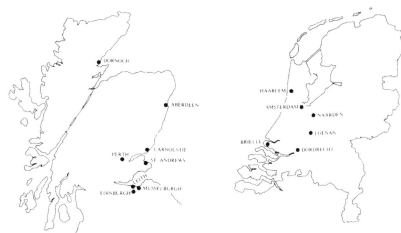

Diagram 159   Places in Scotland and the Netherlands where golf was played prior to 1600.

Note the post as the target.

EARLY DUTCH GOLFERS

stick and a ball made of wood. The high cost of the 'feathery' certainly hindered the early growth of the game in terms of popularity.

When discussing the early history of golf, it is important to mention the role of the Masonic Order in establishing the game on a firm footing. There is evidence of a strong masonic membership in the early beginnings of the Royal and Ancient Golf Club of St. Andrew's, Royal Golfing Society of Edinburgh, Royal Blackheaths. There are three other significant factors worth noting. Scottish golfing holidays became popular, especially with the patronage of the game by such famous people as Earl Haig and Asquith who went on a golfing holiday to Scotland on a regular basis. The game was helped further by the advent of the 'new technology' of that particluar age, the invention of grass-cutting mowers. Before this development the game was played in wintertime when the grass was short. Only then was it possible to move away from seaside to inland links. Another interesting factor was the development of railways. Golf became popular, especially in towns which had a railway link with hinterland regions.

Why did St. Andrew's Become the Home of Golf?

I would advance two reasons, which in my view, were central to St. Andrew's becoming the most important golf centre in Scotland in these early years.

The first important factor must be the powerful and influential group of Freemasons who were enthusiastic followers of the game and certainly were the guiding lights in the early fortunes of St. Andrew's Secondly, the year 1522 is very significant in the annuals of this world-famous club, for in that same year John Hamilton, Archbishop of St. Andrew's, confirmed the right of the community to play golf over the links, only when he was granted a license to breed rabbits within the precincts of the Northern parts of the course. It is interesting to note that from 1522 the people of this famous golfing centre had free golf on all courses in the town up until about 1846.

The Big Breakthrough — "The Ball that Made It".

The big breakthrough in the development of the game took place in 1843 with the discovery of Gutta-percha. It is a milky juice which is obtained chiefly from the Palaquium gutta trees of the Malay Peninsula and, as a substance, was used as insulation for electric wire and submarine cables. It was also used for castings, surgical bandages and even at one time for temporary tooth fillings. It was used for a time, replacing "The Feathery", as a new type of golf ball. At the time, the new ball was cheap, durable, and its discovery was responsible for bringing the game within the reach of those who could not afford "The Feathery". The discovery of 'Gutta-percha' as an opportune time indeed, around about the year 1848. In the preceeding years a sudden diminution in the popularity of the game had occured. Golf had reached its lowest ebb from about 1820-1850. The game had died in Holland; in Britain it was preserved by the enthusiasm and support of the Masonic Order and the wealthy merchant classes, but, certainly, it had become more elitist and more the preserve of the rich, prior to the introduction of the Gutta-percha. It must also be remembered that when "Gutta-Percha" was introduced to the game, golf clubs had to be developed and changed.

1850-1910

During the years after the introduction of this new, less expensive, long lasting golf ball, the game was to flourish and become popular throught all five Continents. Apart from the ball there were other secondary, outside factors which had positive consequences for the game. Close trading links were establish between Britain and those new colonial outposts; the merchant adventurers were also to play a significant part in fostering the game in these far flung corners of the world. A further discovery with regard to improving the ball took place around 1890, with the invention of yet another new ball called the Haskell (the first generation of modern balls), because of its discovery by a Cleveland golfer, called Coburn Haskell.

Historical Landmarks

As you can see, we have been witnessing some significant developments especially during the 19th century. In order to put into perspective historically what actually occurred, let us look at the following synopsis of special events and dates recorded.

1567   Mary Queen of Scots is reputed to have played a game of golf at Seton House in Scotland, shortly after the death of her husband, Lord Darnley.

1641   In Irish history, this an important year. 1641 marks the year of a major uprising which took place in Ireland. The news of the outbreak of war was conveyed to King Charles while he played a game of golf at Leith. The King was being beaten in the game, and as he rushed off on hearing the news, it was remarked that he wished to save his "half-crown rather than his crown".

1658   First reference to the playing of golf in England, it having spread down the East coastline of Scotland, golf recorded for this particular year was played outside London.

1744   The first rules of the game were drafted at Leith. There were thirteen rules drawn up in all.

1780   Royal Aberdeen Golf Club was founded.

1829   The game had reached India with the formation of the Royal Calcutta Club. This was a date of significance in that it was the first club which was established outside of Britain.

1856   The first club on the continent of Europe was established in France, in the Basque Region.

1867   The first Ladies Club was founded at St. Andrew's.

1871   Dunedin, New Zealand, established its first Golf Club.

1874   Royal Montreal founded.

1881   Royal Belfast founded.

1883   Curragh Golf Club founded.

1885   Royal Cape of South Africa founded.

1888   The first golf club established in America at Yonkers, New York, by two Scotsmen, John Reid and Robert Lockhart.

1890   The first golf club founded in Belgium. This same year witnessed the return of golf to its original home, in Holland, where it had undergone centuries of decline and decay. It merely underlines the enormous contribution of the Scots to the game, for yet again, it was a group of Scottish golfers who opened a club and course at the Hague.

1891   Long Island, New York founded.
          Lahinch, Co. Clare founded.

1897   Bray Golf Club founded.

1898   Copenhagen established first club.

1901   Japan established first club.

1904   Gothenburg, Sweden established first club.

1908   Buenos Aires, Argentina established first club.

1963   The year 1963 is significant in that the game had now reached all five continents, culminating in the establishment of the Asian Golfing Association

From our synopsis of special events in the development of the game worldwide, let us focus more particularly on the game in Sweden, Japan and America. In Sweden the game has grown in popularity in recent years with a dramatic increase in the number of courses built, making Sweden one of the strongest nations in Europe. The game in that northern country received a powerful boost from the outstanding athlete, Sven Tumba, who became a superstar and folk hero as an ice-hockey player. On turning to golf, he focused the consciousness of the people towards this new, developing game. It was principally due to his enormous influence that golfing fever became an epidemic, capturing the imagination of millions of Swedes. Today, Sweden stands on the threshold of manifesting itself as a great golfing nation.

The story of Japanese golf is, in many ways, more remarkable. The game is still very much at an embryonic stage of development, and one might say as a national pastime has only taken off in the last 30 years. In a country small in size, over-populated, highly-industrialised, mountainous, naturally whatever land that is available is taken up for agriculture. Consequently, with so little land available for golf course lay-out land on the tops of mountains and other rocky and remote areas were blasted and many multi-stored driving ranges were built near cities of Japan. The most well-known driving range is the Shiba Park in the centre of Tokyo, a three-storey complex.

These really are a substitution for courses and can be better understood when one realises the national importance of every inch of land for cultivation.

In Spain, the craze for golf came about with the developing tourist industry. As tourist facilities were developed for the thousands of tourists flocking to the golden beaches on the Iberian Peninsula, golf courses were as essential a facility as the swimming pool. Holiday tourist were in need of caddies whenever they played a game of golf and it was in this way that Spain's greatest ambassadors for the game took the golfing world by storm. It was through this system that the Miguel brothers, Manuel Pinero and the great Severiano came to the fore. The rest is history.

The man responsible for planting the first seed of golf on the newly-emerging continent of North America was Alexandra Dennistoun. He was born in Edinburgh in the early years of the 1820s and emigrated to Canada about 1874. He was the first founder of Royal Montreal. The establishment of other golfing societies in Canada came about because of the presence of Scottish Regiments who were on overseas service in that part of the Commonwealth in the latter years of the 19th century. Then in 1888, another Scot, a native of Dunfermline, a certain John Reid founded St. Andrew's Golf Club at Yonkers. Willie Dunne, yet another famous son of Bonnie Scotland, built the first course in Long Island. America had been captured. The game was now about to expand and in the short space of no more than 15 years more than 1,000 clubs were established all over the States. One might wonder how, the game came to develop to the degree that it now has in the U.S. There are three important factors which should be considered.

First of all the 1890s was a time of massive economic and material development and nationally this had an important bearing. Secondly, with the advent of television, the new sport was given intensive coverage, just like in Japan, at a time when one of the great charismatic figures of American golf burst forth on the golfing scene, Arnold Palmer. He more than anyone else turned golf into a national pastime and TV Sport. And this brings us to the Third factor and the reason why golf became such a success. Arnold Palmer and his close friend, President Eisenhower more than any other people, helped immeasurably the advancement of the game. Palmer had charisma. He was aggressive, likeable, a risk-taker, adventurous, brilliant as a champion, he personified more than any other sporting hero of all time all that was good in the American personality. He became the hero from humble beginnings. He more than any other person was golf's greatest asset. His close friend Dwight D. Eisenhower, a national hero from his World War II exploits, became one of the great aficionados of the game. He was shown regularly on TV having a game of golf.

No chapter on the History of World Golf would be complete without reference to the contribution made by the all-time greats. Henry Vardon the self-taught champion created his own individual and unique style and technique. His was a major input in elevating the game to a high degree of skill and challenge. Walter Hagen, the flamboyant champion of the cavalier type gave to the sport style, character and sophistication. He will be remembered for his single-handed battle to emancipate his fellow professionals from a lowly status. As one writer so accurately put it, "He brought the professional from the locker-room to the tea-room". It must be remembered that this was a time when the golfing professional was prevented from socialising in the clubhouse. Hagen would arrive in his chauffeur-driven limousine and would order champagne and oysters, having his party in the car park, when refused entry to a clubhouse. Hagen was influenced by the attitude and ethos of Michigan Golf Club where he was the professional. The Fords, the Chryslers were members there, all of them coming from lowly and humble origins. They believed that their fellow man should be judged not by his background, but by his ability, his success. "It is not where you come from but where you are going to that best characterised this new entrepreneurial spirit of these self-made millionaires". The great Gene Sarazen once stated. "Whenever a tournament pro holds a large winners cheque between his fingers, he should give silent thanks to Hagen". Hagen won ten major championships, Sarazen seven.

Bobby Jones, another champion among champions, gave to golf something new. Having degrees in law and engineering, Jones more than any of the stars of his time, best captured in an articulate sense, the demands and challenges of the game. In a 7-year span, he recorded thirteen national titles in the U.S. and in Britain.

The names of Henry Cotton and Ben Hogan represented a new era in golf. The days of the wild and inimitable Hagen were over. In order to be champion, Cotton and Hogan believed that a new commitment, discipline and exhaustive preparation were essential. Hogan was the first to analyse the game in the most fundamental way possible, programming his game in a meticulous manner. In more recent times, Nicklaus, Thompson, Tom Watson, Ballesteros, Trevino and now Langer have heralded a new breed of champion, diverse in personality, articulating their game in divergent respects which in many ways were but a progressing development on the styles and techniques of their illustrious predecessors.

If I were to pick out a personal star among stars I would choose the great Palmer. The career of many a superstar is like a short story, but that of Arnold Palmer has the amplitude of a great novel. Many of the great stars are masters within an accepted mould. Palmer was a breaker and maker of moulds. Moments of beauty in golf just like in any other sport are all the sweeter because they are so difficult, so hard to attain. The beloved Palmer contributed many, many such moments and his humanity struck a chord in the hearts of millions all over the world that was to set him apart from all the rest. Palmer showed that **supreme form** depends as much on charisma and likeability as on titles and championships won.

In this short Historical Tour around the world, it is indeed fascinating to note how in such a short period of time the game set root in so many diverse corners of the world, becoming truly international indeed. The only remaining part of the world where golf has yet failed to take root is within Iron Curtain Countries where the game is still looked upon as an elitist pass-time, which of course is not in keeping with official Ideology. Perhaps in the not too distant future, it will become the one game most capable of establishing that international bond between peoples around the world, whether it be in Peking, Moscow, Dublin, Edinburgh, Tokyo, Copenhagen or Augusta, Georgia.

In summary, let me say that no matter what the rival claims may be with regard to the original home of this wonderful game, whether it was the Scots, the Romans or the French who were the first innovators, but it is to the eternal credit and honour of the Scots that the game was preserved and developed after it had died a sudden and inexplicable death in Holland. There is some truth in Ernest Rewen's belief that the Celts mistake dreams for reality. It might be nearer the truth to state that they sense a world beyond what is commonly known as the real world. Surely that must be the intuition at the heart of the Scotsman's passion for sport, their passion for golf; for above all it expresses the quest for glory in the challenge of field games. It was this enthusiasm, this quest for glory, perhaps the adventurism of their temperament which saw the Scots in the forefront of a great sporting crusade, pioneering the game in different corners or the World. Their love of golf is an enternal testimony to a great sporting people.

History of the Game in Ireland —

Ireland's Oldest Established Clubs

Nobody can be absolutely certain when golf was first played in Ireland. From all authentic records and source material available, there is evidence to substantiate the claim that golf was played in the last decades of the 18th century in the Curragh of Kildare and in or near Bray as far back as 1762. There are records which show that golf was played in an area in the Phoenix Park which was acquired for the game prior to the year 1850. It is noteworthy that from the early period of the 19th century, golf was played in the Phoenix Park by army officers of Scottish regiments stationed in Dublin. Indeed, it is of significance that just like in most other parts of the World, it was the Scottish influence which played a key role in the popularisation and establishment of the game in Dublin and its hinterland environs. However, no official clubs were formed. Consequently, there is no denying the claim that Royal Belfast is the oldest actual Golf Club in Ireland, having been founded on November 9th, 1881.

The introduction of the game to the North of Ireland came about in progressionary stages and was due in the main to the close cultural and trading links between Belfast and mainland Scotland. The first impetus came from a Mr. Thomas Sinclair, who, while on holidays at St. Andrew's became so enthusiastic about the game that he decided on his return to set about establishing and introducing the game to Belfast. In collaboration with a schoolmaster by the name of George Bailie, who was a skilled golfer on the staff of the Royal Academy in Belfast, a circular was drafted calling the first meeting. This meeting marked the beginnings of Royal Belfast and took place on the night of November 9th, 1881. There was an attendance of eighteen people and on arrival a subscription was decided upon. Thomas Sinclair was appointed President and the Hon. Secretary was George Bailie. This early missionary zeal was to contined unabated and soon plans were drafted to commenec work on a 9-hole course for Kinnegar,

Hollywood, Co. Down. In 1884, Jack Simpson became the first professional to be appointed in Ireland. His appointment was sanctioned for a five month period initially. It should be stressed that most of this early pioneering work in the North of Ireland must be largely attributable to the organisational skill and flair of Mr. Bailie. Perhaps, it is easier to understand, when one realises that this great Founding Father of Golf in Ireland was a Scot, having been born in Musselburgh, on the east coastline of Scotland, a town having had long historical associations with the game when at an embryonic stage in its development. With continuing zest, having resigned from Royal Belfast around 1888, he set himself the task of establishing two further clubs, Portrush and Newcastle. It is indeed fitting and appropriate in any History of Irish Golf, that the name of George Bailie, be given a special place of honour.

In these early years of Irish Golfing History, there developed a rather close affinity between Scottish clubs and those newly emerging in North East Ulster. The first in a regular series of visits took place in 1884, when the Perth club came to Belfast and recorded a notable victory over the local side. The year 1885 is also of importance historically. First of all, it was in that year the Prince of Wales came on a visit to Belfast and was made a Patron of Royal Belfast. The derivation of the prefix Royal dates back to that particular visit. In that same year, Royal Belfast made their historic visit to Dublin, where they played a representative team of Army Officers from Scottish Regiments. This particular game was played in the Phoenix Park.

It wasn't until 1925 that the present Royal Belfast clubhouse and new course came into being. The original 9-hole course was considered somewhat restricing, mainly because of the growth in membership and the increased popularity of the game. Former avid followers of football and cricket were now showing a keener interest in the new game. When Craigavad House was sold in 1925 with suitable acreage by the Presbyterian Church, Royal Belfast was to have its final resting place and a new course.

The second oldest Golf club in Ireland is the Curragh Golf Club, Co. Kildare, founded in 1883. The major impetus with regard to popularisation of the game in this part of Ireland at the time, was principally due to the fact that there were many Scottish Regiments of the British Army encamped on the Curragh around these years. The Argyll Highlanders, the Black Watch Regiment, the 71st Highland Light Infantry are among the more well known battalions who were instrumental in bringing about the establishment of the Club offically in 1883. The first captain was Lt. Balfour an officer of the 71st

Highland Light Infantry, whose father had been captain of the Royal and Ancient. However, it is important to remember that golf was played in these parts prior to 1883. It is of interest to note that there were many distinguished visitors to the Curragh in these years. It is reputed that Edward VII paid a visit to the course in the 1860s, so also did the Prince of Wales, during his captaincy of the Royal and Ancient. Other distinguished visitors and afficionadoes of the game of golf were the Duke of Clarence, while serving with the Royal Huzzars, and the Duke of Ellinton who was captain of Prestwick in 1851 and of St. Andrews in 1883. Indeed, it is easy to understand how a golfing ethos was established and became a part of the sporting mental climate of the region — the Scottish input was indeed both significant and fundamental.

The third oldest established club in Ireland is Bray Golf Club. As I have already outlined at the outset, golf was played in or near Bray as far back as 1762, despite this however, it was not until 1897 that Bray Golf Club was officially founded. On Friday, 16th July of that same year, a meeting took place in the International Hotel, Bray convened by two golfing enthusiasts, David Stewart and James Robson. This historic meeting was attended by a small group of people, who were to play an important role in the immediate events which brought about the foundation of the club. Negotiations were entered into with Lord Meath for the purchase of land at Ravenswell. These negotiations proved positive as on August 11th, 1897 Bray Golf Club was officially founded. In a short span of time, there were 170 men registered as members, and 96 lady associates. 1898 marked the Club's official affiliation with the Golfing Union of Ireland.

The early 1900s saw the game flourish in many different parts of the country. It was in these early years of the new century when many of Ireland's famed Golf Clubs were established — Portmarnock, Rosses Point, Little Island.

It was in Post-War years after World War II that Irish golfers achieved International acclaim and recognition throughout the World. These achievements, these successes greatly enhanced the progress and development of the game in this country. Jimmy Bruen from Cork in 1946 won the premier amateur Golf crown, the British Amateur Open. In 1947, Fred Daly became the first Irishman to win the World's number one professional golf title, the British Open. Further golfing history was recorded when in 1958 Harry Bradshaw and Christy O'Connor went to Mexico City and carried off the Canada Cup, a trophy which was then competed for by every golfing nation in the World. Ireland staged the Canada Cup at Portmarnock in 1960.

Achievements of this magnitude were to greatly increase the game's popularity and attractiveness as a competitive sporting hobby. Further successes were recorded by Irish Golfers in the Walker Cup and Ryder Cup Competitions which had a notable bearing on the International standing of Irish representations. Joe Carr, one of our most revered ambassadors for Irish Golf, figured prominently in every Walker Cup match against America from 1947-1965.

The game in Ireland presently enjoys widespread popularity, attracting more and more devotees every year. Almost every club has a waiting list of intending members. The growth of Junior competitions has been instrumental in fostering an interest in the game among our youth, thereby ensuring an infusion of new talent into every level of the game. Increased levels of sponsorship given by Irish firms has attracted the cream of English, European and American talent to our shores, adding a new dimension to the status and quality of the game in Ireland.

And with the biggest golf event in the world, 'The Ryder Cup' coming to Ireland will elevate our little 'golf county' to the very top of the golf world.

CELTIC TIGER
COMES TO IRELAND

TWO TYPICAL GOLF LESSONS

Lesson 1

APPENDIX

PROBLEM	ADVICE
The slice	Correct the slice by changing the set-up, not the swing

When a golfer comes to me with a major swing problem, I do not try to change his or her swing. Rather, I change the set-up, as a result of which the player will make (or be forced to make) a completely different swing.

It's as simple as this. A player tells me, 'My problem is that all my shots are high and right, I have a terrible slice.' I know that his swing-plane is much too steep, his angle of attack on the ball is from the outside down, and the actual clubface is 'open' to the swing-line at impact. I explain the need to **change the angle of attack** from 'above' to 'behind', the need for a **more inside, wider backswing,** avoiding the quick left. His tension grip is ruining any chance of a smooth swing. I tell him: 'Do you know that you are gripping so hard, you are squeezing the blood out of your hands and the life out of your game.' If he wants a tidy game he must have a **light grip.** Above all he must **'knuckle down',** that is, show more knuckles on his left hand. This grip change will alter the clubface angle automatically. I insist that he set his left side much higher than his right side — drop his right shoulder down and tuck in his right elbow. Finally, I change his stance from an open to a closed one.

SHOW 'STRONG' GRIP

Every angle has altered. All roads lead one way. I have trapped his body into a position whereby the only escape route is from the inside out. His new (awkward) body position will block any attempt at the outside-in route. The grip change will close the clubface at impact.

I insist that he uses a no. 7 iron and 'tees' the ball up.

Here is the sequence:
- GRIP: change left-hand grip to show more knuckles
- FOCUS on back rather than top of ball (more inside)
- STANCE: closed (again more inside)

Swing/backswing
- Turn more inside
- 'Hood' the clubface on the way back and extend triangle.

Forward swing
- Clear the left side
- Close the door; rotate right hand over impact.
- Do not hit the ball any more, instead learn to 'hook' it down the fairway.

Lesson 2

PROBLEM **ADVICE**
Lack of distance Increase the distance by
adding 'leverage' to the
swing.

A golfer comes to me for a lesson. She is
unhappy with her game. She is elderly and
associates the 'ageing' process with her loss
of distance. I know instantly that her swing
lacks 'leverage'. The problem is compounded
by the fact that the more distance she
loses, the more she feels she must force the
shot. Hence she makes a violent attack on
the ball. The swing is very short, hurried,
steep, and a frustrating one with little return
for the 'effort' involved.

I always start the lesson by asking 'Do you
know you have a clubhead?', and to drive
the point home I say, 'You know it's not an
ornament you have at the end of the stick.' I
stress the need to **regard the club as a
machine.** The grip end is only the 'holding
end', the clubhead end is the 'working end'.
I tell her she must **'work the stick'** a lot
more, to manipulate, to activate the
clubhead end. If you consider your hands for
a moment, it is very obvious that the fingers
have far more manipulative powers than the
palms. I insist on her achieving **much more
'finger grip',** to knuckle down — a lighter,
lower finger grip. I demonstrate the 'bending
of the shaft' on the ball by strong
'waggling' of the clubhead — bending the
lower end of the shaft.

I encourage her to **swing more,** to increase the length of her backswing by excessive wrist-work, to 'overswing'. I show her how the swing is 'pumped' — how power is pumped into the swing. I egg her along with phrases like 'Your old swing made you look as if you were in a phone box!', 'You are in such a hurry to swipe the ball...you must be double parked outside the range!' and 'If you are going to miss it...you might as well miss it with a good swing!' All the time I am endeavouring to unlock her swing, to unlock the power so that it can be released on the forward swing.

LEARN TO RELEASE TO CLUBHEAD

On the forward swing, above all I encourage her to really let that clubhead go at the ball through impact, to feel the clubhead win the race to the ball. I show her the **ideal impact position** — the clubhead is way ahead of the hands at impact. It is as if somebody has hooked her hands back at impact, pulled the handle back and allowed the head fly through. You only need power *once* in the golf swing — at impact. The strong right hand can be a killer in the backswing, but **strength is a tremendous asset if you use it at the right time.** I demonstrate the right forearm 'power kick' at impact.

A longer, slower, freer swing will become self-generating and powerful. Sam Snead once remarked that to play your best golf 'you must feel that your wrists are oily'.

'QUIT WHILE YOU'RE AHEAD'

Pine Valley is probably the toughest golf course in the world. It is often referred to as a 184-acre bunker. It terrifies golfers.

Woody Platt, a gifted local amateur, started on the toughest course, a par 4, 427 yards (390.5m), and managed a birdie 3. This was no easy task as the hole bends sharply to the right after the tee shot to a green that drops steeply into trouble on both sides and to the rear. He played a 4 Iron second shot.

Hole two, 367 yards (335.5m). The tee shot must carry 180 yards of sand peppered with flash-traps along its right side. The green of course is elevated and completely surrounded by sandy wasteland. Woody hit a 7 Iron second shot directly onto the hole for an eagle 2. (Three under after two holes.)

Par 3, 185 yards (169m). Strictly a one-shotter as there is nothing between the tee and the green but sand, sand, sand. The green tilts sharply from right to left downhill. If the player misses this green, a 6 or 7 is possible. Woody solved the problem by the single expedient of a hole-in-one. (Five under the card.)

Hole four is a very long par 4, 461 yards (421.5m). A blind tee shot with the hole swerving very sharply to the right. There is sand everywhere. Woody Platt struck a Driver and 4 Iron and then holed a thirty-footer for a birdie. (Six under the card on one of the toughest golf courses in the world.)

The first four holes make a full circle back to the clubhouse. Woody now faced the prospect of playing the fifth, one of the toughest par 3 courses in the world. A huge bunker lies in front of the green, falling steeply to the right onto saplings and undergrowth. As the hole is 226 yards (206.5m) long, he would have to play a Driver. Before proceeding, he decided he needed to bolster his spirits with a drink in the clubhouse while he contemplated the task ahead.

He never came out of the clubhouse! This is a true story.

GLOSSARY OF GOLFING TERMS

Ace
The ultimate stroke in golf, a hole in one.

Albatross
A hole completed in three strokes under par.

Arc
The path which the club takes through the swing.

Better-ball
A game in which two partners play as a team and the best score is counted. Also called *four-ball*.

Birdie
A hole completed in one stroke under par.

Blind (hole or shot)
A blind hole is one where the green cannot be seen from the tee. A blind shot is made when a high object prevents the player from seeing where he/she intends to hit the ball.

Bogey
A hole completed in one stroke over par. A double-bogey is a hole completed in two strokes over par, and so on.

Bunker
A hazard filled with sand.

Bye
The number of holes left to be played when a match is finished.

Caddie
A person who carries the player's clubs.

Casual water
A temporary pool of water on the golf course. When the course is waterlogged after heavy rain, the player is permitted to lift and drop the ball clear without penalty if it is lying in casual water.

Chip
A short shot to the green.

Concede
A hole is conceded when one player has played so many shots that it is impossible for him/her to win or halve it with the opponent. A player may also concede the opponent's putt if he/she feels that the opponent is certain not to miss. Concessions take place only in match-play.

Dead
Used to describe the situation when the ball lands so near the hole that it is all but impossible for the player to miss the putt.

Divot
The piece of turf that is sometimes removed when the ball is struck. All divots should be replaced to avoid damage to the course.

Dormie
In match-play, a player is dormie if he/she is as many holes ahead as there are holes left to play, for example, if a player were three holes ahead with three to play, then this player would be dormie three.

Draw
The spin imparted to the ball so that it moves gradually from right to left.

Eagle
A hole completed in two strokes under par.

Fade
The spin imparted to the ball so that it moves gradually from left to right.

Fairway
The cut portion of the course between the teeing ground and the green.

Flagstick
The pole, usually with a small flag attached, that is placed in the hole to provide the player with a target. Also called the *pin*.

Fluffed shot
When the player strikes too much ground.

Fore
A shout of warning to anyone on the golf course indicating that the ball is travelling in their direction.

Four-ball
See BETTER-BALL.

Foursome
A form of golf with two partners per team, but instead of playing their own ball as in better-ball, the partners play alternate shots with the same ball and drive at alternate holes.

Free drop
Under certain conditions a player is allowed to drop the ball away without penalty. Check the rules of golf if in doubt.

Green
Each putting surface on the course.

Greensome
A form of foursome in which two players play as a team but each player drives and then the team decides which ball to play in alternate strokes for the remainder of the hole.

Grip
The position of the hands on the club and also the top part of the club where the hands are placed, which is usually covered in rubber or leather.

Ground under repair
Ground which has been repaired by the green-keeper. The area is usually marked by a small notice.

Halved
A hole is halved, or a match is halved, when the opponents are level, either in relation to strokes taken at each hole or at the end of a round.

Handicap
The figure allotted to every player, denoting the average difference between his/her score and the par of the course.

Hanging lie
A downhill lie.

Hazard
A bunker, ditch, stream or pond.

Hole
The target on the green into which the ball must ultimately fall. The hole is 4½ inches (11.43cm) in diameter. Also refers to the full distance between tee and green.

Holing-out
Striking the ball into the hole.

Honour
The preference given to the player whose turn it is to drive first. The honour on the first tee can be agreed, but thereafter it goes to the player who had the lowest score at the previous hole. If a hole is halved, the player with the honour retains it.

Hook
A shot which moves sharply in flight from right to left.

Hosel
The point at which the shaft of the club enters the clubhead.

Knuckle down
Term used to describe the four-knuckle grip.

Ladies' tee
The teeing ground used by women golfers, usually placed some distance ahead of the men's tee.

Lateral water hazard
A ditch or stream which, when viewed from the fairway, runs parallel to a hole instead of across it.

Lift and drop under penalty
If a ball has to be lifted because it is impossible to play it from where it lies, the player is permitted to lift and drop under the penalty laid down by the rules.

Local rules
The rules of golf apply everywhere the game is played, but all clubs have additional rules on certain points pertaining to the layout of the course.

Loft
The angle at which the clubhead lies in relation to the shaft.

Lost ball
Players are allowed five minutes to look for a lost ball, after which time they have to deem the ball lost and play another.

Match-play
When players play against each other individually or as a team.

Medal-play
When the player counts the number of strokes taken during the round. Also called *stroke-play*.

Niblick
A golf-club with a heavy head and wide face, used for lofting.

Obstructions
Objects, either movable or immovable, which prevent the playing of a shot.

Out of bounds
When the ball is hit over the boundaries of the course or hole, thus incurring a penalty.

Outside agency
Any person or animal not involved in the game who obstructs or moves the ball.

Par
The rating allocated to a hole or to a course, based on the terrain, the length of the hole and the level of difficulty.

Partner
The person with whom one plays.

Penalty
When a shot finishes in a lie from which the ball is unplayable, out of bounds or lost, then a penalty is incurred according to the rules. Penalties can also be incurred for infringement of the rules.

Pitch
A high, lofted shot played from near the green.

Playing out of turn
In match-play, if a golfer plays out of turn either from the tee or fairway, then the opponent may request that the ball be called back and the shot played again.

Playing preferred lies
See WINTER RULES

Power fade
Long shot which flies slightly to the right at the end.

Pull
A shot that flies directly to the left with no slice-spin; to hit a shot directly to the left with no hook-spin.

Push
A shot that flies directly to the right with no slice-spin; to hit a shot directly to the right with no hook-spin.

Putt
The stroke used on the greens and played with a putter.

Round
To play a round is to complete all the holes on the course, usually eighteen.

Rub of the green
Interference with the ball that is attributed to fate.

Score-card
The card that is filled in by golfers in stroke-play. It has to be filled in by the player's partner, and checked and signed by both players.

Set-up
The player's position at address.

Shank shot
Ball struck with the shank of the club.

Short game
The term used to describe shots played in the vicinity of the green.

Sky shot
Very high shot.

Slice
A shot which moves sharply in flight from left to right.

Stroke
The striking of the ball.

Stroke-play
See MEDAL-PLAY.

Swing-line
The direction of the swing.

Swing-plane
Angle of swing in relation to the ground.

Take-away
Backswing.

Tee
The wooden or plastic peg on which the ball is placed prior to driving off. Also the teeing ground.

Tee-markers
Metal or plastic objects used to mark the forward limits of the teeing ground.

Tempo
Speed of swing.

Through the green
The term used in referring to the whole area of the course *except* the teeing ground, the putting green and all hazards on the course. The term is also used when a player hits a shot too boldly so that it runs over the back of the green.

Top
Ball runs along ground.

Trap
Also called a bunker.

Winter rules
Special rules for play during the months when the course is wet or frost-bound. Winter rules allow for the ball to be lifted and cleaned and then replaced adjacent to its original position but not nearer to the hole, without penalty — thereby lessening the damage to the course. Also referred to as 'playing preferred lies'.